MW00942438

"You saved my life. Those four words '*You have a choice*' ... I will never be able to truly express how thankful I am."
— Dezi M., *State College, PA*

"*The Best Advice So Far* pulls you in with its relatability. It's not one author telling you how to live; it's a journey of shared experiences and insights delivered in a funny, real way that forces you to reflect on your own life in a positive and uplifting manner."
— Sullivan C., *Denver, CO*

"Filled with insightful and engaging anecdotes, this book certainly lives up to its title. This is an incredible book that you will return to time and time again."
— Ryan G., *Boston, MA*

"Reading a chapter from *The Best Advice So Far* is a similar experience to having lunch with a wise and kind best friend. I finish each section simultaneously encouraged and enlightened, but never with the feeling that I'm being lectured to."
— Paul H., *Dallas, TX*

The Best Advice So Far

Also by Erik Tyler

TRIED & (Still) TRUE

and coming soon

You Always Have A Choice

The Best Advice So Far

Erik Tyler

Cover photography: Michael F. Dubois

For booking information:
booking@TheBestAdviceSoFar.com

3rd Edition
USA

*For my grandmother, Beatrice Kwiatkowski,
and for my dear friend, Carlotta Cooney,
whose lives have spoken volumes.*

CONTENTS

Contents

Contents

THANKS AND ACKNOWLEDGEMENTS

Mom, for believing that I could, for reading along the way and for telling me that every chapter was the "best so far";

Holly and Richard, for embodying the heart of unpretentious wisdom, sharing and storytelling;

Maddie, for lending a critical eye and encouraging spirit at just the right time;

Michael, for stepping into the picture – the big one and the small;

Dylan, for sparking the idea in the first place;

Chad, for inspiration, for helping me stay focused, for invaluable feedback, for friendship, and for living a book-worthy life;

Bud, for being a rock and for illustrating with grace what it means to express the heart of a truth with few words; and

Dib, for reminding me constantly who I am and why it all matters.

My sincere thanks, as well, to every person so far who has read or listened or pondered or asked a question or checked in on things along the way. You are as much a part of this book as I hope it might become of you.

FOREWORD

If you are lucky, you will at some point in your life experience a "friend at first sight." You meet someone for the first time, and there is a particular twinkle in their eye, or you laugh so hard at the same moment, or they say something that drills deep into your soul. And you know—you will love them forever.

It's rare and it's beautiful.

This very thing happened to me just about 20 years ago. I was at church, of all places. It was at the end of the service during the last hymn, and as usual, there were the many mismatched voices around me—some OK and many not OK—when remarkably, I heard one that stood out. I mean really stood out! I stopped singing and just listened. This voice was talented, but it was more than that; whoever this was, was just enjoying singing and creating new harmonies with a very old song. It was lovely. When it was over, I turned around to see who this might be. And there it was: the twinkle… the laugh… and then the soul drill.

I was smitten for life.

Since then, I have continued to experience love from this wonderful and rare individual. But more than that, I have been privy to his unusual wisdom, his incredible compassion and his unrivaled understanding of the human.

What you are about to read is a wonderful snippet of practical life wisdom from the most interesting and talented brain of my best friend.

Enjoy…

Dibby Bartlett

The Best Advice So Far

**Courage is doing
what you're afraid to do.
There can be no courage
unless you're scared.**

*Eddie Rickenbacker, WWI flying ace
and Medal of Honor recipient*

Preface

ABOUT 500 YEARS AGO, a guy named Nicolaus cleared his throat and announced to the world that the universe does not, in fact, revolve around us. However, eons before Nicolaus dared to speak up, the facts were the facts. It did not matter what important people thought or knew or wanted to believe. The earth has simply never been at the center of the cosmos.

As dinosaurs tromped around the planet, the principles of flight that now allow several tons of metal to take off and get airborne—were just as true. It just took us a while to figure them out.

Truth is true, whether we know it yet or not. Truth is true, whether or not we choose to believe it or acknowledge it. Kick and scream all you like. Truth just is. The best any of us can do is to discover it, to better understand it, and to explain it in such a way that others can make some sense of it with us.

A few months back, some kids I mentor set up an online discussion page in my honor. The name is something like "I Wish I Had a Pocket-Sized Erik." Crazy kids. On this page, they recount with one another meaningful advice I've shared with them. It's one of the hazards of mentoring, that some kids inevitably get starry eyed and think you are magical and tell their friends that you started "The Wave."

I want to make it clear at the outset here that I take no credit for inventing the advice in this book, any more than Copernicus can take credit for changing the orbits of bodies in space. If there is truth to be found in the pages that follow, it has always existed. Truth is. I've just collected it. Repackaged it. Added some new bells and whistles along the way.

With some of the advice in this book, I can recall the moment when it was passed along to me. Some of it I gleaned from books. Still other trinkets of the advice found here I'd swear I got from a certain close friend— who will swear she got it from me. I'm known to have a knack for analogies, and I guess I've wrapped advice in those mental images so often over the years, that for many, it seems to have originated with me. Honestly, in most cases, I don't remember exactly how I came into the advice. I think I just pay attention in life and take note when I see patterns of truth.

Some may argue that individual bits of advice in this book do not as stated constitute advice at all, but rather something closer to a principle or proverb. It's true that, where clarity or impact would be improved by so doing, I chose to favor brevity over strict adherence to grammatical structures.

The relaying of truth is a collective effort. It's not terribly important where we hear it, only that we respond and change accordingly. I trust you will find your own gems of wisdom here. My hope would be that some of it becomes so much a part of your everyday life and philosophy, that you too will wind up passing it along to others, even if you are unable to remember quite where you heard it first.

Preface

Questions for Reflection and Discussion:

APPENDIX page 321

CHAPTER 1

Choice

WHAT I AM ABOUT TO SAY is foundational to all that will follow in this book. Don't race through it. Spend some time with it. Read it several times if you must. If you can really internalize it and live it, it could quite literally change your life.

First, as is my way, I'd like to start with a story.

I mentor teens. I've done so for more than three decades. By mentor, I do not mean that I've joined an organization and agreed to spend a block of time each week with a teen. While I certainly encourage and see the value in this type of commitment, my mentoring takes a broader scope. At any given time, I'm investing in twelve to twenty young people on a personal, day-to-day basis.

A couple of years back, I had about a dozen seniors I was mentoring. We'd sort of formed a band of brothers back when they were freshmen. It was now April, and many of the guys were suddenly and simultaneously falling apart. Frantic calls at all hours. Lengthy, erratic emails. One of them had even asked to come over near midnight. When he arrived, he sat on my couch shaking and in tears, trying to explain that he had been having repetitive nightmares and was generally panicked at all times. I listened as he gushed for a while. Then I looked at him sagaciously. "I see.

I think I know exactly what's going on." His eyes widened, as if he were sure I would tell him the term for some rare form of psychosis, which he would readily have believed he had.

"*What is it?*" he pleaded, tears still falling.

"You're graduating," I replied, smiling.

In addition to hanging out one-on-one or in smaller clusters during the week, this entire group of guys met together on Mondays at my place for dinner and open dialog. That particular week's discussion point was a given. I've always thought it negligent somehow that society doesn't better prepare seniors for this phenomenon: the emotional upheaval that accompanies stumbling headlong from childhood into adulthood. It seems as obvious and necessary a topic as the birds and the bees. The simple fact, I told them, is that sometime during the three months before or after graduation, when faced with the end of life as they know it and the beginning of life as they *do not* know it—high school seniors have a period of what feels a lot like mental breakdown. They wander through an unpredictable maze of fear, lethargy, mania and other erratic moods. I told them that, as odd and scary as it may feel, this was completely normal. And that set their minds at ease that they weren't, in fact, going crazy like Great Aunt Bertha.

As we went around the circle, pressed in close along the olive sectional in my living room, each of them shared how they had been feeling, relieved to hear that they weren't the only one. Until we got to Chad.

Chad was different. He was charisma incarnate. And while he listened attentively to the others, offering encouragement and good advice, when it came to his turn, he just couldn't relate. "Gee," he said, all smiles, "I just don't feel *any* of that. And I can't imagine why I ever *would*! I'm excited about college. I'm comfortable with new people and situations. I can't wait to graduate and get started!"

I didn't want to dull his shine. And, if anyone were of the constitution to escape senior panic, it was Chad. But I did want him to be prepared, should it creep up on him later. "That's terrific!" I said. "Just keep it tucked away, in case it hits later on." He shrugged and let it go with a noncommittal "OK."

Graduation came and went. Chad was bubbling over with enthusiasm. He even staged an ostentatious stumble and trip across the lawn as he went to receive his diploma, eliciting a few colorful but good natured words from the principal, who apparently forgot his microphone was on. Chad's graduation party was the hit of the summer. True to his prediction, he remained deliriously optimistic and excited about heading off to college, where he would follow in his father's footsteps, having enrolled as a pre-med student.

I helped him pack the day he headed off. I actually think it was a far tougher day for me than it was for him. I stood in the driveway as the family drove away, Chad waving from the window like a lunatic and shouting back, "I love you, Papa!" (one of his many nicknames for me).

A few days later, I was out having lunch with a friend when a text came through. It was Chad:

Really not doing so hot.
Need to talk.
Call if you can.

I excused myself and called immediately. The voice that answered was barely recognizable. Chad was hoarse and sobbing. Hard.

"Tell me what's going on," I invited.

Chad stumbled over his words, choking through the torrent of tears. Everyone he'd encountered at college was "fake," he told me. No one thought he was funny there. He was on a campus of thousands and felt completely alone. His professor for calculus was Bulgarian. He couldn't understand her, other than that she had made it clear that she really didn't want to be teaching this class, but had been made to by the higher-ups. He was presently curled up in fetal position on his bed in a dark dorm room, finding it unimaginable that he could get up and go to the next class, let alone continue for the long haul at this desolate campus. His world was crumbling. His dreams were over.

It was the first week of classes.

I welled up as he let it all drain out of him. It would have been pitiful had it been anyone, but being Chad—perpetually cheerful Chad—it was all the more heart wrenching.

"OK, Chad," I said when his words had run out, "remember that conversation we had about the panic that hits everyone? It's hitting you. It's normal. You just hit yours a few days late. It will pass. I promise."

Whimpers on the other end of the line.

"Second, you need to go and drop this calculus class

today. It's your first semester. Four classes is fine. You'll feel so much better."

Chad sniffed. "Really?" Something like hope was breaking through. "I can just *do* that?"

"Yes, Chad, you can do that," I said with gentle authority. "You can drop or change every class if you want, and it's still early enough that you won't be charged a cent to do it."

"Yeah, then I'm going to do that. I just didn't know I could. That will be great."

As we talked about Chad's other classes, it seemed he wasn't thrilled with many, even those not being taught by less-than-willing Bulgarians.

Finally, I asked the pivotal question. "Chad… *why* did you choose pre-med?"

He paused. "I don't know," he finally replied. "I guess—my dad and I just always talked about me being a doctor like him, and I guess that seemed fine to me. I couldn't think of anything else I wanted to do, so I just went with that."

"I see. How would you feel about changing that major to something you will actually *enjoy*?"

Chad didn't say anything, but the sun may as well have been shining through the cell phone. "You know what?" he chirped. "*I hate pre-med! I hate science!*" We both laughed openly, even through our sniffling.

We decided that each of us would separately look through the handbook at all of the majors offered by the university. We'd circle anything that we thought was a better possibility, given Chad's personality and interests. The next day, we compared notes. Chad was ecstatic.

Every ounce of despair had been replaced with joy. Among a handful of others, we had both wound up double circling this long shot of an option, but one that just seemed so... *Chad*: Human Services/Rehabilitation.

It was settled. He was changing his major.

"I don't know what my dad will say," Chad chimed, "and I know that it won't pay anything close to a doctor's salary. But I'm *so excited* about it!" He clamored on about the great class lists and the cool professors and the opportunities available to students in this major.

As it turned out, Chad had a great talk with his father. His parents wound up being the biggest supporters of his new major. And, not only did Chad change his major, he began to change the entire campus. He founded a unique club of which he was the president, a club that continues to this day and whose mission is to take positive social risks. And both he and the club have garnered lots of notice. He was featured on the radio and in the newspapers. He met with high administrators who were eager to back his efforts, and even wound up catching the personal attention of the president of the university.

Nice story. But what does this have to do with you? Well, you see, even an ultra-optimist like Chad fell apart and was completely overwhelmed and despondent, because he'd forgotten a very important truth. He was immobilized, because he believed in that space of time that life was *happening to him*, and that he had no say in the matter. Yet, once he was reminded of this key truth, he not only rebounded but began to take the world by storm.

THE BEST ADVICE SO FAR:
You *always* have a choice.

Chad did not need to be a doctor. There was no rule that said he must struggle through a schedule of classes he hated, or even that he needed to remain at that university. Chad had choices.

If you don't accept this truth—that you always have a choice—if you don't remember it and *live it*, then you are left to play the part of the victim in life. You begin (or continue) to live as if life is happening to you, that you are powerless, oppressed by your circumstances. But, if you truly change your mind set to believe and live out in practical ways that, in every circumstance, you have a choice—now, you open a door for *change*. Instead of living as if life is happening to you, *you* will begin to happen to *life*. You will begin to realize the difference that one person—*you*—can make, that you are an agent of change in your own life and in the lives of others.

Don't misunderstand me. I'm not saying that we get to choose everything that happens to us in life. We do not choose abuse, for instance, and we can at no time choose to undo those things which have happened to us in life.

We do not choose illness. We do not choose when or how the people we love will leave us. Or die.

We *do*, however, have the choice of how we will *respond* in every situation, even the hurtful ones. Instead, so often, we pour our frustration and anger into those things we can not change, rather than investing that energy into the many choices that we *can* make from that point forward.

I saw this painted on a classroom wall recently:

HARDSHIP IS GUARANTEED.
MISERY IS OPTIONAL.

I devote a whole chapter to this concept later on in the book. But for now, let that sink in. In the worst of circumstances that life may bring, you always have the next move. You have a choice.

In grieving, will you choose to close yourself off from others? Or will you live with more passion and intention, realizing the precious nature of life?

Will you let the abuser rob you of continually more hours and days and years of your life, through bitterness and anger? Or will you take the steps to thrive and live in the now, using your experience to help others do the same?

So it is with any advice. It is always your choice to try it out. Or to discard it. You can skim the pages of this book, mentally assenting or theoretically debating with me about why such-and-such wouldn't actually work in real life. Or you can come along for the adventure, try some new things, and see what happens.

The choice is yours.

Questions for Reflection and Discussion:

APPENDIX page 323

CHAPTER 2

Negativity

I KNOW SOME PEOPLE—too many of them, really—who seem to be in a perpetually bad mood. These people drift along, frequent sighs having replaced anything akin to wind in their sails. They have somehow managed to find the worst jobs with the meanest bosses and most backstabbing co-workers. Asking "How are you?" is met with a tragic roll of eyes and sucking of teeth. The quaver in the opening word of the reply—"Well …"— indicates that you will not escape any time soon, but will be subjected to a lengthy and painstaking tale of woe. It seems that whenever I run into one of these people, they have coincidentally just that morning had some streak of catastrophic bad luck or other. Despite their obviously tragic circumstances, they report that their unfeeling family and so-called friends continue to criticize, hurt and reject them. Traffic jams, illness and botched orders at the drive-through are attracted to these people like dirty cosmic magnets.

I feel bad for these people. But it is not because of some plight with which they've been cursed. I feel bad for them, because they have unnecessarily spent so many unhappy years with a continual knot in their stomach.

THE BEST ADVICE SO FAR:
✗ Being miserable is a choice.

Some of you just got mad. My short piece of advice feels like judgment to you. You're telling yourself that I don't understand, that this is a generalization, that your circumstances are far more complex or a special case.

At least hear me out. Then you will have all of the information, even if it is only to better fuel your anger toward me in the end. Might as well make your fire a doozy.

Or maybe, it will be the unimaginable—happiness. Freedom. Peace. If you will at least entertain the possibility, then you've already chosen to put your foot in the door to a better place.

I recently saw a short video about a man named Nick. As the video begins, the camera is zoomed in on Nick's face. He is a young, handsome man with a cool Australian accent. (Then again, to Americans, an Australian accent is always cool.) His voice is warm and friendly. You instantly like Nick. You know somehow without a doubt that, whatever he may be about to say, he is not acting. Nick announces that he likes to swim, boat, play golf. It almost seems like a dating advertisement. After the short list, which manages to exclude "long walks on the beach," Nick finishes his greeting: "I love life. I—am happy."

The camera zooms out. Nick is on a couch. Nick has no arms. Or legs. Well, he has something there where a leg should be—one small misshapen appendage, which he later refers to as his "chicken wing."

Nick's list of things he loves to do quickly takes on

new meaning from this angle. In a montage sequence, we see Nick on the grass in front of a soccer goal. A ball goes flying over his head into the net. "I wasn't ready!" he exclaims, with a feigned look of childlike excuse. Next, we watch as Nick runs—yes, *runs*, without legs—down the field. He balances a soccer ball on his head far longer than I can. He sloshes down a waterslide. Surfs. Steers a motor boat with his chin. Dives into a swimming pool. Plays golf (again, far better than I can).

But the purpose of Nick's video is not to illustrate some one-in-a-billion scientific anomaly. There are no doctors' testimonials, saying, "We don't know why this man can do these things. It should be impossible given his condition." The purpose of Nick's video is to tell others that being miserable is a choice. And that, conversely, happiness is also a choice. Nick is an international motivational speaker who tells his story so that the very same advice I've given you here has a voice that's difficult to argue with.

But it's still the same advice. True is true.

Nick doesn't paint some Pollyanna picture of his life. We see aides having to pick him up and move him onto a stage or an interview chair. He talks openly about having tried to drown himself in a bathtub at the age of eight, because he saw his life having no possibility for happiness. He would never be married. No one would love him that way. He was a drain on his parents and society. Nick had every circumstantial reason to be miserable. And for a while, he was.

Understand that his circumstances didn't change. He did not get prosthetic limbs. He still needs help in the bathroom, I'm guessing. But something changed, that much is certain. He took the exact same circumstances he'd been handed and *decided*, "If I am going to live, I am not going to live like this." He did not get happier after learning to run or swim. He learned to run and swim, because he decided to start being happier. And happiness breeds hope. He has found a purpose for his life—successfully encouraging hundreds of thousands of people to believe that life is what you make it. That you can always get back up and try again.

Nick is not an isolated case. I know many such people. A friend of mine, Anindaya, has been deaf and blind since childhood. He was not born deaf and blind. He lost his hearing gradually, due to a degenerative condition. He lost the sight in each eye in separate, random accidents in his native country of India. Talk about grounds for bitterness! But he is one of the happiest people I have ever met. He travels the world, unaided except by his dog. He completed an advanced degree and holds a high-ranking teaching position. He is an inventor. He is probably the smartest person I know. And he is married and very much in love.

Maybe this is a good time to bring it back to you. If you've got the miserable bug bad, you probably read those stories and felt some negative emotion. *How did they figure out how to be happy when I can't? I'm a terrible person. I'm selfish. So I guess I deserve the miserable life I have. And, man, am I miserable. Just this morning, I blew a tire…*

And off it goes down that path again.

I was just talking with my niece about a woman we both know. I commented to this mother about how impressed I was with her toddler's memory. "He's a bright one!

He's sitting in there quoting the movie we watched last night, line for line!" In an Eeyore-like voice, she replied, "Yeah. Great. That's because he's seen it a million times. He drives me crazy."

Now, is her two-year-old intelligent, exhibiting solid memory and language skills at an early age? Or is he obsessive and annoying?

My best friend Dib is famous for putting it this way: "The only prize for being the most miserable is... [*deliver next lines with zealous enthusiasm and a gasp of delight*] 'CONGRATULATIONS! You're the Most Miserable!' [*applaud here, then extend invisible interview mic*] "Tell us—how does it feel? You must be *so proud!*"

The nub of it is that there is no gain to being miserable. You're just miserable.

I remember a story I heard once, about a young mother baking a ham. She cut substantial-sized portions off the end of the ham and set them aside. Then she basted the remaining center portion, dressed it, and placed it in the oven.

"Why do you cut the ends off?" her inquisitive six-year-old daughter asked.

The mother paused, then replied, "That's just the way we always did it!"

"But why?" pressed the little girl, expectantly.

"Run along and play," the mother replied. But she was bothered at her own lack of any real answer. Her family *had* always done it that way. She called her own mother.

"Mom, I'm baking a ham and I cut the ends off, as usual. But... why *did* we always cut the ends off?"

There was a silence on the line, followed by, "I… don't really know. We just always did it that way in my family."

The call ended there, but the burning question lingered. The young woman now called her grandmother.

"Hi, Grandma. I have an odd question. Why do we cut the ends off the ham before we put it in the oven?"

"Goodness me," replied her grandmother, "I can't imagine why *you* do it. I only did it because my oven was too small to fit a whole ham."

Consider this carefully. We do virtually nothing in life without some sort of perceived gain. A man trapped by a fallen boulder while climbing endures the horror of cutting his own arm off with a small knife, because he believes there is a gain. Survival. Likewise, we complain, focus on the negative, or respond with sarcasm because there is a perceived gain.

Understand that I said *perceived* gain. Like the young mother in the anecdote, we often get ourselves into situations where we have long since stopped asking what the gain is. However, if we were to spend some thoughtful time answering this question, we may be forced to realize that the end result we were after isn't being achieved. Maybe it has *never* been achieved. And that means we've simply been wasting a whole lot of precious energy that could have been expended in more productive ways.

Maybe for you, this answer to the question of gains will rise to the surface: "I want people to pay attention to me. I never got attention as a kid except for when I was very sick." And so somewhere along the way, sickness—and the collecting of other dire circumstances—became your only hope for being taken seriously and getting the attention a child craves. A helpful realization. But ask yourself, "Am I, in fact, getting more affirming attention from people with my complaining and negative outlook?" The answer is likely no. The answer is more likely that people actually avoid your company or don't often call looking to spend time with you. The intended goal is not being reached.

My aim in this particular book is not to give a case-by-case rundown of all psychological possibilities for what unachieved goals are driving each person's negative emotions and perceptions. It is only to say that there is ample support and research, not to mention countless testimonials, to say that circumstances are not the problem. Choices regarding focus and behavior are. And those can be changed, with diligence. And perhaps a little help from others. I add my own life to the testimonials, and I hope that some of the principles in this book will provide solid suggestions for change.

So where do you start? How do you change what may perhaps be a lifetime of feeling like a victim?

Old habits die hard. They won't change overnight. That much is sure. But they *can* change.

The first step would be to accept that you have become a negative person, and that life or other people are not to blame. This is also the start of embracing that you are part of the solution. Not quite convinced that your problem is all that serious? Ask the three people closest to you. Don't lead the witness, using phrasing like "You don't see me as a negative person, do you?" Ask neutrally. Border on begging for an honest response: "I need to ask you something. It's serious and I need you to tell me the truth. I will not argue with whatever your answer is, I just need to know what you think. Do you see me as a negative person?" Then just listen. Be aware that, from people who love you, the answers you get may be tempered: "What do you mean by negative?" or "I might say you're more serious than negative exactly." Take anything but "No, of course not!" as a "Yes, you tend to be negative."

Breathe. Here comes the hard part, that will bring you face to face with finding out what those perceived gains of yours are. *Tell the people in your life that you are committing to stop being negative. Miserable. Sarcastic. A complainer.* Tell the people to whom you complain most. Tell them that you are resolved not to dwell on negative things any longer, but to focus on the positive. Give them permission to call you out on it when you slip. If you really consider doing this, you may find yourself thinking things like, *I can't do that! If I tell them, I won't be able to _____ anymore.* What you fill into that blank is likely your perceived gain. *I won't be able to get my kids to do what I want them to do anymore. I won't be able to pass the blame for my own failures anymore. I won't have a reason for people to feel bad for me anymore, and that's the closest I feel to loved.*

But again, ask yourself, is your perceived goal being met by the negativity anyway? Likely not. The kids ignore you when you gripe and nag. Others aren't keeping you from the consequences of your shortcomings. Complaining doesn't leave you feeling loved.

So, commit to your new course of action, tell people, and then set a new goal. An achievable goal. Spend time with your kids. Make it your goal to listen to them and understand what's important to them. Make it your goal to gain new job-related or interpersonal skills. Make it your goal to spread cheer and hope to others. As soon as you realize you are getting negative—even if it is only in your mind—stop yourself and admit it. If you are in conversation, admit it out loud: "You know what? I just realized I'm complaining and focusing on the bad here. I'm really trying to be more positive. So, I'm not even going to finish that story."

Don't give in just because the other person offers that "you have to vent sometime" or "it's OK with a good friend like me." It isn't OK. Even if they are content to listen to it, complaining isn't helping *you* to achieve your goal of peaceful and happy living. It is just keeping the old cycle going—the cycle that you are now committed to breaking.

Understand here that being negative isn't an all-or-nothing state. I consider myself a very positive person, but I still have my things that pull me toward moping or complaining. Just the other day, I was running this chapter by my friend Chad, who is probably the most positive person I know. And still, we both were able to notice in one another areas or times when we give in to being negative. There is always room for growth, for redirecting wasted energies into more positive pursuits.

I'd also like to say that, like Nick, you may have legitimately difficult circumstances. But Nick realized at some point early on that what he wanted was arms and legs. A normal life. And it became clear to him that being sad and angry wasn't going to give him those things. So he changed his goal. He decided that, rather than pining for the "normal life" of those who have all their limbs, he would pursue a different goal. A life of *purpose*. *That* goal was achievable, with specific action. And having positive, achievable goals, paired with a specific plan of action to reach them, will change our outlook on life.

Questions for Reflection and Discussion:

APPENDIX page 325

- Commit to one negativity
- Stop focusing on negative, but on positivity blc its
- If you can't achieve something change your goal
  not in the cards for you

CHAPTER 3

Positivity

S O, YOU'VE LOOKED in the proverbial mirror and decided that you complain or become negative more than you'd like. You're committed to change. Great! But now what? When you feel that black bubble rising inside, do you stuff it back down by sheer will power? Do you just grin and bear it when things go awry? Is the goal simply not saying negative things and hoping it changes how you feel?

It is certainly true that misery loves company, in the sense that negativity only breeds more negativity. The more we speak negative words, the more we perceive the world and other people through a negative lens. It stands to reason (as well as research) that speaking fewer negative things causes our outlook on life to be less negative.

But that is not the end goal, to simply be "less negative." While living at dead center may trump living in a funk, the real goal is to learn to live more positively—to actually see the beauty and wonder that already exists in the people and circumstances around us.

THE BEST ADVICE SO FAR:
Practice positivity.

This does *not* mean "Buck up, camper!" or "You just need to pull yourself up by the bootstraps!" The goal is not to behave in a more positive or palatable manner outwardly. The goal is to actually *become* more positive on the inside.

No one who is great at anything became so by simply deciding to be great. Likewise, you cannot just decide to be more positive. It takes *practice*. And practice is work.

Every cloud has a silver lining. This may at first sound like some platitude that your great grandmother might have doled out, back in the days when people borrowed cups of sugar from neighbors and thought clean humor was funny and didn't seem to know very much at all about how complicated the world really is. I'd like to challenge you to dust off this saying and to practice it. Practice it like an athlete practices in preparation for the Olympics. Write it on a sticky note and put it on your dashboard. Set your phone to send you a reminder midway through your day. Heck ... frame it and hang it on your wall.

Sounds nice in theory. But how does it work in a real-world setting?

First, consider it a challenge. A contest. You win if you can find the positive side in each seemingly negative situation. (If it helps, you can keep track of your score on that sticky note that's on your dash.)

I'm going to tell you a story. I like stories. This story is true.

I woke up one morning this week and went to take a shower. When I turned on the water, it hissed and sputtered, glugging out a pathetic amount of water. Then it just dripped, emitting a high-pitched whine. I turned the lever off, fuming. *I pay for hot water, and now I'm going to be late for my ten o'clock appointment!* I picked up the phone and stabbed in the numbers for the property management office. When the office attendant answered, I tore into him.

"*Why* do I have no hot water?" I said ominously. "I have someplace to be in a half hour."

"I just got a notice on that, sir. Let me see…" He fumbled through some papers. "Yes, they're replacing your furnace today, sir. It shouldn't be more than two hours."

"*Two hours?* You have to be kidding me!" I exploded. "You can't just shut off people's water without notice! Replacing a furnace isn't something that just springs on you. How hard of a job would it have been to put a notice up yesterday to let us know?"

The man stumbled over himself apologetically, "I'm very sorry, sir. I don't know why there was no notice. I'll speak to maintenance and find out why that happened."

"Well, speaking to maintenance about why it happened isn't going to get me a shower right now, *is it*? So now, I'm going to have to call and cancel my appointment, because you people can't manage a simple thing like notifying your community when you're going to turn off our water."

"I'm very sorry," he repeated. This was followed by an awkward silence.

"I have to go and—figure out how to fix this mess. So, goodbye."

I sat on the couch, seething. Should I drive up to the office in my rumpled clothes and bed head, to really make my point? I texted my next appointment: "Idiots shut off my water without notice. Have to cancel. Sorry." Then I began to plan a letter to the CEO of the management company, expressing my outrage at the injustice.

OK. Stop.

Isn't this how we get? It doesn't seem any silver lining was found here. Yes, the circumstances were inconvenient. Yes, the management should have had more foresight. But my reaction is still my choice.

I'm pleased to inform you that, while the initiating circumstances were true, my reaction in the above account was completely fabricated. This is how it really went down.

I woke up one morning this week and went to take a shower. When I turned on the water, it hissed and sputtered, glugging out a pathetic amount of water. Then it just dripped, emitting a high-pitched whine.

I turned the lever off. *Hmmm.* I had an appointment at ten o'clock. I picked up the phone and dialed the management office.

"Hello. My hot water seems to be off. Do you know what's up?"

"I just got a notice on that, sir. Let me see…" He fumbled through some papers. "Yes, they're replacing your furnace today, sir. It shouldn't be more than two hours."

"Two hours. Yikes! I have an appointment in a half hour. I didn't see a notice about it," I replied.

"I'm sorry about that, sir. I don't know why a notice wasn't put up."

"Well, at least they're fixing the broken heater," I said. "It's been on bypass for a week or so since the last one went, and it'll be good to have full heat and pressure back. Thanks."

"Again, I'm sorry for the inconvenience," the man repeated.

"No problem. Not your doing. Thanks for the information. I've been around the world and seen some things. I should be able to handle a cold shower."

We laughed and then said our goodbyes.

I sniffed under my arm. Decent. Didn't need a full shower, I decided.

I grabbed my face wash, shampoo, a washcloth and a towel, and headed for the kitchen sink, which is deeper than in the bathroom. I turned on the cold water, running the washcloth under it. Really cold. It would certainly wake me up. Plus, cold water tightens the skin. Bonus.

I washed my face quickly, then bent down to put my head under the faucet. I was suddenly reminded of summers when I was a counselor at a camp at the northernmost part of Maine.

The bathrooms were rustic and kids used to get up at four and five in the morning to vie for the limited hot water. Anyone who got up after six took an ice cold shower. I was certainly wily and tenacious enough to get up before anyone else and take a long, hot shower. But I enjoyed thinking that, by taking a cold shower, I was sort of "giving" the hot water to one or two of the other kids. I loved that camp and my campers.

By now, I had rinsed the shampoo out and was toweling off my hair, smiling at the memory of individual kids I'd had over the years at that camp. I wondered where they were now.

Having skipped a full shower saved me time. I made my ten o'clock appointment in plenty of time.

You see, the circumstances didn't change. I just found the silver lining. And that changed the events that *followed*.

Where I could have begun the day stewing and clenching my jaw, my day was off to a great start.

On the Fourth of July this year, I got caught in bumper-to-bumper traffic in town. I had just gotten off the phone with my friend Chad who lives about a half hour away, and we'd decided I'd come down to watch an impromptu late-night movie. I had somehow forgotten that our town had fireworks this year. Once I was swept into the stream of cars around the rotary, I was stuck. It quickly became a virtual parking lot, and there was no escaping in either direction. I called Chad: "I'm going to be *very* late!"

Here again, I had a choice. Many people around me were already laying on horns and throwing arms in exasperation. *Silver lining*, I thought.

I looked over at the car going the opposite direction, stopped beside me. A boy of maybe six was in the back seat, twirling his pink glow necklace, smiling, oblivious to the traffic.

I put on the radio. I took out my cell and began to text encouraging notes to some of the kids I mentor. Many texted back with equally affirming thoughts. Some of the texted conversations really got ridiculous. I laughed more than once. I would say I managed to send positive notes to a dozen or more kids. They felt like they mattered. I had used the time wisely. Forty minutes had passed and I finally approached my escape route on the right—a street that would have been a three-minute trip under normal circumstances. After taking a few back roads, I got to Chad's almost an hour late. He couldn't have cared less. We watched our movie and stayed up talking after that. It was a terrific night.

It could have been a miserable one. I could have boiled with irritation in my car, being mad at the world. I could have decided that I was sick of it all by the time I reached the turnoff, and just canceled plans with my friend and drove home mad.

Traffic and plumbing issues aren't the worst things, you may argue. What about the *really* hard stuff that life throws at us. Where's the silver lining then?

I read a story once of a woman who was placed in a Nazi concentration camp for helping to hide Jews. She tells of how, in addition to the daily horrors she and her family endured there, her bunker of women had an outbreak of fleas. For many of them, this additional trial threatened to be the proverbial last straw. But this woman pointed out that, since the outbreak, the cruel guards had not come into their area and hassled or abused them, fearing that they would themselves be exposed to the fleas. It turns out that she and the other women had relative peace and freedom in their bunker, because of the infestation. She was adept at finding the silver lining.

My grandfather passed away in the spring. Twenty of us were around his bedside when he passed, one hand on him and another on my grandmother, his wife of nearly seventy years. It was surreal and somehow beautiful. I sang at the funeral. It was the hardest thing I think I've done. What good can come of death?

Through the planning and wake and services, our extended family bonded in ways we never had before. My grandparents had six children, who all have children. Our living line extends to great-great-grandchildren. There is a twenty-year age gap between my mother and her youngest sister. So, while I've seen many of my younger cousins at a family event here or there and we've been cordial, I've never really known them. My grandfather's death opened doors for us to know each other. In fact, if you read the acknowledgments, you'll have noted that the whole idea for writing this book came out of a graduation card I wrote to my much younger cousin, Dylan, with whom I connected in a new way during the circumstances around our grandfather's passing.

Silver linings are everywhere. Make it your personal challenge to find them. They will surprise you. And the world will begin to look different.

Practice positivity. Practice makes perfect.

Questions for Reflection and Discussion:

APPENDIX page 327

Every cloud has silver lining
Next Difficult event, actively seek out silver lining

CHAPTER 4

Starting Again

I WISH YOU HAD KNOWN my best friend's mom, Carlotta. She passed away more than a decade ago now. It's still hard to believe. When I visit with my friends, in the family home by the marsh where they still live, it feels more like Carlotta has just left the room for a moment than that she is gone. The yard and the garden are still very much hers.

Carlotta's very essence was family and laughter and irrefutable common sense. She observed much and spoke little. And when she spoke, you listened.

She was my friend.

When Carlotta passed away, after a long battle with cancer, she left much behind. She left a legacy. She also left some tangible things. I'm not referring to items of material worth, though we're still finding that some odd thing or other that's been lying around or hanging on a wall forever is worth a fortune. For the purposes at hand, however, I'm talking about her writings.

Carlotta wrote a book. It's nothing short of breathtaking. It alleges to be a cook book, filled with recipes that, for the last fifteen years or more, have defined Thanksgiving, Christmas and summer parties for me. But the recipes are really just a clever excuse to draw the reader into the moments taking place *around* the food, with family and friends. If you haven't lived in New England, Carlotta's book is likely the closest you could come to feeling what it is like. Her personal anecdotes are truly sentimental without being the least bit sappy.

Carlotta wrote more than a book. She wrote on everything, from books to pictures to objects. We have yet to find all of her notes, I'm sure. Among her scratches and scrawls, she left a little piece of paper in her bedside table. As best we can figure, she wrote it while she was at her worst with the cancer. That's important.

I have a copy of this handwritten note, along with a picture of Carlotta in her health. She is turning to look at us from the kitchen sink, smiling in a way that makes you feel like wherever she was in time is where you want to be. I have these two items in a simple, wooden picture frame in my house. The three pieces of advice she left in that note are in the running for my most often quoted and most treasured.

THE BEST ADVICE SO FAR:
You have to start from where you *are*, not from where you *wish* you were.

My alarm went off at 4:30 one morning. Yes, I actually set it for that downright silly time, despite having gone to bed mere hours before at 1:15. Why? I was headed to the gym.

Please don't get the wrong idea about me. I am not a gym rat, or whatever they're calling it these days. I enjoy being fit and healthy. It does as much for my mind as for my body. But I am by no means obsessed. I know—4:30 looks like a time that only the obsessive would choose to workout. The fact is, that is the only time my workout partner could manage in his schedule, between family, work and tending his several properties. I'm more of a ten-to-midnight guy myself.

At any rate, that morning was the first time I was to work out in about three weeks. (I told you I wasn't obsessed.) I had thrown my back out some weeks ago, for no reason I can figure, and had been waiting to no longer feel the twinge that threatened to send me to the floor. My workout partner, coincidentally, had also been unable to work out, due to unusual circumstances with his properties and having had family in town for a couple of weeks.

So there we were. It was still wet from last night's rain. If the sun was up, we couldn't tell through the clouds. We got out of our cars in the lot to the gym—alongside only three other vehicles—and headed into the gym together. We made small talk about our love handles and how we might need to be rolled from room to room. In all honesty, we're in decent shape. But just as honestly, starting back after a three-week absence is tough. *Really* tough. We started with thirty minutes on the elliptical. I checked the readout twice, sure that I'd punched in the wrong settings. This couldn't be our usual numbers. I was winded within the first five minutes. The virtual hills felt more like virtual mountains. I sighed and smiled, turned toward my friend, and quoted Carlotta's words again: "You have to start from where you are, not from where you wish you were."

After our thirty-minute warm up, we headed off to start the first press. The temptation was strong—temptation to load those bars with the same weights we'd been using three weeks ago. Maybe it's a guy thing, but I tend to think not. It feels a little like admitting defeat if I don't perform "where I wish I was" as opposed to "where I am."

Still, Carlotta's little piece of advice, firmly engrained by now, won out over temptation. We cut our presses each by fifty pounds, followed by dropping our dumbbell weights by five or ten pounds, as well. Even with these concessions, my numbers weren't what they had been at higher weights just three weeks ago. Understand that I *could* have loaded up the bars to be where I left off weeks ago. I might have gotten some reps out of it. But I would have been discouraged. I would be in pain later today. And, even if I did manage not to throw my back out again, 4:30 tomorrow morning would feel a whole lot like torture.

Life is filled with situations where we face discouragement because we are not where we wish we were. Weight. Finances. Relationships. Trying to break old habits. When we find ourselves in these moments, we have a choice. Starting from where we are means more than admitting weakness and begrudgingly adjusting our actions to accommodate. Starting from where we are is an attitude. It is a decision to be happy without being complacent. It is focusing on what I have accomplished today, instead of what I have not. It is celebrating that I am still in the game.

So, you're not a fitness buff. Or you are, but you never miss a day. Let's see how this plays out in some other areas.

You've got a huge term paper due in two weeks. You've known about it for a month, but done nothing on it as of yet. To live "where you wish you were" is to berate yourself for not having started earlier, burdened with the knowledge that you should be through with your research and note cards, and well into your first draft by now. Wishing you were further along uses up mental space that needs to focus on where you *are*—which is at step one. So, you let go of wishful thinking and ask, "What do I need to do right now to get started?" Maybe that is as simple as choosing a topic. Maybe it is finding your sources. Or maybe it is writing out a plan for what you will do each day until the paper is due, as if it were only assigned to the class today. When you accomplish each step, congratulate yourself that you are that much further along than you were when the day started, rather than continually reminding yourself of how far behind you are. That is starting where you are.

Or let's suppose that one night you are struck with the hard realization, in that quietness just before sleep takes you, that you don't know your son anymore. You've worked too much. You haven't made time for him. And now your relationship with him is reduced to grunts in passing, or barked commands about school work and chores. Trying to start where you wish you were may make you overzealous. You may attempt to immediately instate family meetings, pressuring him to cancel plans that he's already made. Or you may push to have a "real conversation" out of the blue, making things awkward for your son, and perhaps resulting in your feeling rejected when it doesn't turn out as you imagined. Starting where you are may be as simple as saying, "Hey, I know I haven't been around much for you lately, but I'd like to try to change that." Starting where you are is accepting an awkward, "Uh...OK" without being offended.

Celebrate that you've realized you want to change, that you took a first step, and that your son heard you.

Not long before that gym outing, I had lunch with a friend whose marriage was all but over a year ago. Focusing on where he wished they were would have left him in despair, putting undue pressure on them both, and most likely divorced. However, by taking small steps from where he was instead of where he wished to be, he's now able to report that he and his wife are really enjoying one another again.

As my friend and I left the gym that morning, the clouds were just starting to burn off. "Hey, we're here, right? A lot of people aren't," he said. He headed for his truck as I got into my car. Just before I shut the door, he turned back and shouted. "See you tomorrow?"

Workout over, I sat down to write. I'd had a few days of writer's block where this book was concerned, as well as some eye strain. I'd hoped to be seven or eight chapters along at that point. It's one of life's many intriguing mysteries, that this was the chapter that would break the dry spell and urge to be written that day. One more chapter completed.And I made the choice to celebrate.

Questions for Reflection and Discussion:

APPENDIX page 329

CHAPTER 5

Unfairness

WHILE THIS BOOK by no means needs to be read sequentially, I do recommend reading the previous chapter and acquainting yourself with my friend Carlotta. It will make the advice that follows all the more meaningful.

I had a friend in my younger years who was plagued with the notion that life was not fair; hence, he was a chronic complainer. His brother was a vagrant, his mother was ill, and his father was unknown. When he spent time with friends who were happy or around fairly functional families, he rarely left expressing that he had enjoyed himself. Rather, he would say that he was depressed, reminding himself and others of all that he had *not* been handed in life.

Every boss he'd had was a complete moron who continually asked too much of him. He frequently called in sick or quit, in search of the ever elusive job that was going to treat him as he deserved.

When money was tight and bills were due, my friend was like a starved coyote, pacing and growling. Most often, instead of paying what he could, he would go out and spend what he did have on things he did not need, justifying the purchases with the fact that, given how hard everything was for him, he had a right to at least have *some* happiness.

On one such occasion, in addition to having maxed his credit cards, he was now in a situation where he owed me an increasingly large sum of money. Rather than try to squeeze blood from a stone, I tried to help him come up with some better strategies and perhaps some long-term financial solutions.

He had dropped out of college, having failed most of his one semester of classes. When I asked if he'd thought about going back to school and getting a degree that would open more doors for higher paying employment, he sniffed at me in disgust. "That's easy for you to say," he hurled. "School was a breeze for *you*. You barely even had to study. Well, we can't all be born geniuses." I reminded him that I'd earned my degree, through years of hard work. I pressed that, maybe here a few years later, he would find he had more motivation to stick with it this time around. He retorted that the reason he'd flunked out was that his teachers were boring or mean. He even proposed that the reason he'd failed gym that semester was due to the unreasonably early start time—of 8:00 in the morning.

I tried to shift gears, suggesting various part-time jobs he might consider in order to start getting out of debt. He escalated even further, his face contorted with sarcasm and his words a torrent. "You know what? I'm busting my butt at minimum wage already, while you work part time and make—what?—at least five times what I do! It's all so *easy* for you," he spat. "If you weren't doing what you do now, you could make tons of money in computer programming. And if that didn't work out, you could sing or play the piano for a freaking *hour* at a wedding and make my whole paycheck. Everything's just handed to you on a silver platter. I mean, you could literally be a Chippendale dancer if you wanted to, for God's sake!" He was red-faced and heaving.

Though I'm certain the timing couldn't have been worse, I was unable to keep myself from laughing aloud at this last comment.

"I'm serious!" he countered. "You got the perfect mind, perfect looks, perfect body. And what did I get? The shaft, that's what I got!"

It was no use trying to continue the conversation at that time, so we left it alone for the time being.

The next time we talked, I gently brought up our last conversation. I told him that I was trying to help him and encourage him, not make things worse for him. I reminded him that most things worth having in life don't happen by lot or luck. They involve making certain choices and investing time and hard work. Somehow, of all the topics on the table, the turn of events led to my inviting him to come along with me to work out at the gym that afternoon, offering that you have to start somewhere.

At the gym, he got on the treadmill beside me. I didn't want to discourage him, so I told him I'd just go as long as he did. Within five minutes, he was complaining. Before the ten-minute mark, he jabbed the button to stop the machine. "I can't do this," he huffed. We tried some dumbbell curls. I helped him pick an appropriate starting weight. After a few reps, he quit and just leaned back on the rack, waiting for me to finish. The next set was a repeat, with him doing five or six reps and then stopping to watch me. I suggested he lower his weight and try to get a few more reps. He muttered something about feeling ridiculous enough as it was, and refused to lower the weights. Moments into the third set, he growled angrily and clanged the weights back into the rack. "I'm done," he snorted, and stomped off to the locker room.

Back in his bedroom, he took off his shirt and looked in the mirror at himself. Front. Side. Some attempt to flex something or other. Then, hurriedly, he pulled his shirt back over his head. "This doesn't even work. It's no use. I just don't have the kind of body to be able to do that."

And so, after fifteen minutes of his first attempt at a workout, he'd decided that Fate was against him yet again.

THE BEST ADVICE SO FAR:
The sooner you realize
that life is not fair,
the happier you will be.

Recall that this advice was practiced and passed on by a woman who was experiencing the most difficult time of her life. She was a kind and loving wife, mother and friend. It was not *fair* that she had cancer. But she accepted this. And with that acceptance came a sense of peace, even purpose.

You see, those who expect life to be fair behave as though some cosmic scale is being balanced on behalf of each person. For every difficult thing, they are owed an equally easy thing. For every pain suffered, they have somehow earned the right to expect a comparable pleasure. As the hard knocks stack up, resentment and impatience mount, begrudging the Universe for being so lax in evening the odds in their favor.

And so they sit, unwilling to budge from crumbling docks, demanding that their ship come in.

In short, this belief that life is supposed to be fair immobilizes us. It leads to that victim mentality that I mentioned in the first chapter on Choice. The fact is, life is in large part what we make it. Bad things happen. Happy people have merely learned to accept the bad parts as a given, to shrug them off quickly, and to capitalize on the many good things around them.

So let's say I'm lonely. I've tried being friends with certain people, but they just aren't interested. Or I asked someone out and they turned me down. It seems everyone else has close friends and lovers except me. If I believe that life is supposed to even out, what will I do? I will reheat last Friday's take-out and eat dinner alone, sulking and wondering when my phone will ring. Furthermore, I will feel that, when that phone rings, it had *better* be someone who will be my soul mate immediately, never let me down, and always be available—in order to make up for the years I haven't been granted what everyone else has.

But—if I accept that life isn't fair, I will not wait for things to change. No one owes me anything. If I want friends or a relationship, it's going to be up to me to put in the effort. I'll have to go out there and be friendly, even if I'm rejected at times along the way. If I want to spend time with the friends I do have, I won't be keeping track of who called whom last and waiting for it to even out. I'll just pick up the phone and call.

If I don't like my weight, I won't bemoan those skinny blankety-blanks who can eat a whole pizza and never gain an ounce. I'll accept that, though it may be harder for me than others, getting to where I'd like to be will not come via some cosmic scale suddenly tipping in my favor to even things out in my life, but through a decision to change my eating habits and stick to an exercise regimen.

I have seen people overcome seemingly insurmountable odds, and go on to thrive. And I have seen those with plenty of potential wither away in the briar patch of bitterness. In essence, it all comes back to choice. Life will be perceived as good or bad based on the choices we make at each turn, not on some unseen and unpredictable system of pluses and minuses. In short, if I want my life to be different from what it is, I'm the only one responsible for bringing about that change.

Questions for Reflection and Discussion:

APPENDIX page 331

CHAPTER 6

Happiness

IF YOU'RE POKING THROUGH THE BOOK at random and have no idea who Carlotta is yet, consider reading this chapter as a unit with the previous two. You may well understand what follows without taking my suggestion; but as I said in starting the preceding chapter, I believe you'll find that the advice here will take fuller shape within the context of the person who passed it along to me.

I spent eight years of my life committed to one girl. My heart was hers and hers alone. Truth is, I pined after her even longer than that.

Now, I say I was dating her. She would say I was sometimes dating her. Or rather that she was sometimes dating me. Or at least that we were sometimes *something*. I'm not sure I even knew what dating was back then, I was so young when it all started. We attended the same school. We didn't really talk about what we "were" very often, but everyone knew that we were *something*. At least they told me they did. Most of the time, I was OK with being that nebulous *something* as long as I could be with her. Smell her perfume. Write locker notes to one another. Talk to her often. Back when land lines and one service provider were all we had, my parents forced me to get a separate line; after all, she lived a whole forty minutes away, and any calls outside of a twenty-mile radius were considered long distance. The result was regular three-hundred-plus-dollar-a-month phone bills.

Sometimes, in early high school, when I'd falter—doubt *us*—I'd venture bringing up what exactly we *were*. She'd look me in the eyes and tilt her head toward me, a wicked little smile forming. She'd say something like, "Why do we have to put words to it? Why is it so important that everyone else have a label for us, when *we* know what we are? Isn't that all that's really important?" And I'd think, *OK, I think that means we are what I think we are. Phew! I think.*

As high school graduation drew near, these semi-reassurances were no longer enough. While I was away on my senior trip to Disney World, I confided in a friend during one of those senior-trip, late-night talks, that I was going to break up with this girl when I got back. I loved her, but I knew somewhere in my head that I should not go off to college as an unspoken *something.* It tore me apart. But I was steeled to do the deed. When I returned, I called her. "We need to talk."

She cut right in. "Hi! Welcome back! I really need to talk to you, too. Can I go first?" Hearing her voice started to corrode the steel. I didn't want to do this. But I had to. Still, I could do the gallant thing and let her speak first.

"Yes. Sure."

She sighed in a way I'd never heard from her, like for once, she was actually unsure of herself. There was no wicked little smile behind her voice this time. "Listen…

I've been thinking. I… haven't treated you very well. You've… been amazing to me for four years, and I've never given you a straight answer about what we are."

My heart felt like it was not going to keep up. Was she finally going to tell me I was… *nothing* to her? Why had I let her speak first. I didn't want to end things hearing that it had all meant nothing!

She continued, "You are everything I could ever look for in a guy. And… this is hard for me to say, but… I really want to be with you. *With* you. Like commit. Boyfriend and girlfriend, and tell everyone."

My eyes pounded in their sockets. All of the sadness and rejection I'd felt was forced out every which way by a rush of overwhelming elation! It was one of the few times in my life that I was quite literally speechless.

"Erik? Are you there? I… know that seems like it's out of the blue, but… it isn't. When you were away, I really missed you and I thought, I don't want to be without you in my life. Ever."

I've since imagined that the voice that finally emitted from me was low and sexy, perfectly calm. In reality, I'm sure I sounded like the frog prince before the royal transformation. "I want that, too."

"Oh, good!" she whispered, relieved. "I thought for a second there that you'd given up on me. Which I would have understood. I don't know how you didn't give up on me earlier." Silence. "Oh!" she giggled warmly, "You said you had something you wanted to talk about, too! I almost forgot. I was so nervous about my thing. What's up?"

I was literally crying with joy and relief. I felt dizzy. "Oh, nothing. I just wanted to talk about… the same thing, actually. But we said it all."

We talked a long time that night, keeping the children of the good folks at the phone company fed.

Graduation was the following weekend. I didn't have my own car yet, so graduation day was to be the first time I'd actually see her after that, though we talked by phone every day in between. I wanted that day to be perfect. The graduation itself was obscured by this new development in things.

Brace yourself for what is to follow. Decide *now* that you will not send mocking emails to me. Be mature. Be understanding. Be amazed.

I had never kissed her.

In fact, if I'm being completely honest, other than during games of Truth or Dare, I'd never kissed anyone yet. Not in a romantic, I-mean-it kind of way. Ah, tender seventeen.

In today's world where grade-school kids I know are "going out" or talking about protection, I'm sure I seem like the biggest freak. We were raised a certain way, and I'd been after her since before kissing was a thing for us back then. I'm not sure about all the ingredients that led to this reality. Religious repression, my own perfectionism. But, those are the facts. And now I was horrified. Would I be a good kisser? What if I did it *wrong*? We didn't have the Internet. I couldn't just Google [how to kiss].

I decided to write a song. I'd already written her songs before this. One was called "Special Place in My Heart." Another was called "Fairy Tale." Breath-taking, I know. What's more, for the very first time, I am going to reveal to you, my reading audience, some of the lyrics to the latter.

This is World Premiere stuff. Hang onto your hats, kids.

> *I used to think that unicorns were fairy tales,*
> *That knights in shining armor don't exist;*
> *Magic seemed as silly as the rest did,*
> *And dragons were a fable, just a myth.*

> *I doubted that there was a well of wishing*
> *Or a fountain that could make an old man new;*
> *But I believe in all of these and more now—*
> *You made my fairy tale come true.*

I'll give you a moment to let the chills subside. There's more, of course, but my talent agent has cautioned me against revealing all the wonder at once.

It's important to note here that, while I had written this girl several songs, I'd always *given* them to her on cassette tape (if you don't know what that is, do a quick Internet search). "Here. I wrote you something." I never sang or played them for her live, and I never listened to them with her. It was write, pass, part, chat later.

This time, I was going full monty. This time, I was going to write the song of all songs. And I was going to sing it to her, at the piano. Live, baby. And then—*then*— as the last notes hung in the air, I was going to seize the moment. And kiss her.

Graduation was a blur. I was Valedictorian. I said some things I presume I worked on before saying. I got some awards. I don't remember what they were for. The whole time, in between marching and the speeches and applause, I just kept running through those lyrics to my song.

I air-played the chords on my knees. Over and over. It had to be perfect. It had to be!

The diplomas had been passed. The caps had been thrown. Goodbyes were said. Tears were shed. And the last lingering conversations slipped out the doors. I had told her—my *girlfriend* (oh, the joyous ring it had!)—that I had something for her afterward, but I had to give it to her at the school. I was in high standing with all of the staff, and so I'd borrowed keys to the building. We walked into the empty and silent auditorium together. The humidity from the crowd was dissipating and it was beginning to cool. A lone spotlight was on, directly over the black grand piano. I led her by the hand to a place beside me on the bench. My ears were ringing with nervous anticipation. I said nothing.

I began to play the opening chords of the song. My song. Our song. It was called "Saying Goodbye." It had just the right amount of melancholy parting at my going off to college and hopeful resolve in our newly confirmed and public relationship. And so I played. It sounded good. It was all just as I'd imagined it would be! It was happening! Only—I'd forgotten the words to the first verse. For what seemed an uncomfortably long time, I played those first chords over a few times, trying to act like it wasn't a mistake. And then, my salvation! The words flooded back into my head. I sang it out, getting quiet and loud and raspy at all the right parts.

The last few notes hung in the air. It was *déjà vu*. The time was here! I leaned toward her. I made nice, soft lips like I'd practiced. And… contact! Oh the bliss! Oh the rapture! I was engulfed in the heat rising from my collar and in her perfume. Then we drew apart.

And a long, slimy string of drool formed a drooping trapeze between our mouths, finally breaking to swing down and slurp against each of our chins.

I am not lying to you. I wish I were.

We did our best to quickly and discretely tend to things. We didn't laugh. We never spoke of it again.

That summer was magical. I left for college completely confident that, when I was through, we would marry and live happily ever after.

I was later to find out that my confidante from that late-night senior trip chat had tipped her off when we got back, that I was going to call things off for good. That explained the sudden change of heart. Or at least words.

Unfortunately, college was a repeat of high school. She knew I was hooked, and her commitment became less verbal. Less public. Less. She went to a school fifteen hours away, and our talks dwindled. Early on, she reneged on the *boyfriend-girlfriend* thing and said she wanted to go back to just "knowing what we were." I couldn't let go. That one summer had given me the taste of happiness that being with her could bring. We could have it again that way. She was just nervous. She still loved me. I needed her to love me, or I could not ever really be happy.

I waited. She dated. I didn't know. The spring before she graduated, I visited her during break at her house. I came to tell her that either she committed—like it had been during that summer years ago, once and for all—or it was over. And yet I was still prepared to marry her if she did commit.

She told me she'd been seeing other people, as far

back as high school. She said she hadn't told me because she didn't want to hurt me. And she informed me that she was engaged to someone else. They married that summer. It was over.

THE BEST ADVICE SO FAR:
If you're expecting someone else to make you happy, you never will be.

Now, before you think this advice is a bitter refrain, hear me out.

I might rephrase Carlotta's advice this way: No one can *make* you happy. You see, happiness is a choice. I chose to allow myself to be happy only if I could have this girl, and have it be in my fairy tale way. I deluded myself, by choice. When I look back, I saw signs. I *chose* to ignore them. I can admit this now.

I repeat: happiness is a choice. It does not happen to you. You choose it. Or you choose to bypass it. As I said in my chapter on choices, this does not mean that we always choose our circumstances. But we choose what we *do* with those circumstances. I chose to fixate on a dream that was not real. And so I chose not to be happy. There were countless reasons to be happy all around me, and I missed them during those years. I see them now, as clear as Christmas. But I missed them then.

The fact is, not only can no one *make you happy*, no one can *make you mad*. Or jealous. No one can make you love them. In each case, the responsibility for these choices lies solely with us.

Let's take anger. How often do we find ourselves saying, "That person just makes me so angry!" And, so, in our minds, our mood is necessarily *their* doing. It is out of our control. They have the control. But consider. When that person criticizes you or argues with you or leaves dirty socks on the floor, would it make someone else angry? Would it make *me* angry? If the power were coming from that person, it should. A critical person in your life might even become critical of me directly, and it will likely not have the same effect on me as it has on you. It may even have no effect whatsoever. But again, if this person held the power to "make you mad," they would logically hold the same power over everyone. And they don't.

Or what if the sock dropper or barker were a senile old man in a nursing home you were visiting. Would his socks *make* you mad? If he growled furiously at you, shaking his gnarled fist, "Mabel! You've burned the stew again, you old cow!" would it *make* you mad? I don't think so.

So, if the power of anger is not emitting somehow from the person, nor from the actions themselves, where does it come from?

It comes from within ourselves. We *choose* to allow ourselves to give in to anger. Or we can choose not to.

Still not convinced? Who hasn't experienced a mother in the throes of screeching bloody murder at her kids when the phone rings. Does she chance missing the call? Or pick up in a rage, shouting, "Whoever you are, *leave me alone!* My rotten kids are driving me crazy!" No. And you know this to be true—she picks up that phone, dire threats still issuing forth, and magically becomes June Cleaver, chiming "Hello…" in musical tones. Maybe that was your mother. Maybe you *are* that mother. But herein lies further proof that we *can*, in fact, choose where being angry is concerned. Even mid-swing.

Now, while no one can *make* you happy, there are certainly people in life with whom it is easier to choose happiness! I highly recommend spending most of your time with such people where possible. And there are people with whom it is harder to make that choice. Likewise, there are people with whom it will be easier to resist choosing anger, and people with whom it will be more difficult. But the truth remains: whether easy or difficult, the choice is ours.

And accepting this is far from a bitter refrain! It is freedom. Someone else isn't running—or ruining—your life. Not your lover or spouse. Not your parents or your boss or your kids. They simply don't hold that power. Only you do.

Questions for Reflection and Discussion:

APPENDIX page 333

CHAPTER 7

The Limelight: Stealing

T HERE I AM AT MY SCHOOL DESK, eight years old. I'm not the least bit self-conscious that I'm dressed in olive and mustard plaid, or that I'm sporting tortoise shell, horn-rimmed glasses and a bowl cut. The matter at hand is all-consuming. The teacher—gaudy, red beads about her neck and glasses bearing an uncanny resemblance to my own—has thrown the gauntlet. She has asked a question. And I must answer.

I can't quite explain the urgency at work in my little body. But my hand is up. Way up. It's the uppest hand in the room. I've achieved this by standing in a sort of way that still *looks* as though I'm sitting (to actually have left one's seat would have meant a scolding or worse), yet it gives me just that slight advantage. It's quite the trick. You have to lean forward just a bit to pull it off, supporting your weight on your desk. Yet you've got to maintain the right balance. If you lean too far forward, you lose the height of hand that straighter posture affords.

I also appear to believe that I am more likely to be called upon to answer if I suck air through my teeth as though I've just burned myself on a hot surface.

And I *am* hot. I am hot—because I know the answer.

I. Know. And this I must proclaim.

But, alas! The teacher has done the unthinkable. She has called on Robbie instead of me. I deflate into my seat, trading the height I'd reached for a sullen slump.

Why is this so important to me? It's true that I like the attention of being called on. But that's certainly not all that's going on here. The majority of my thoughts look something like this.

At least I'm sure she noticed me and knows I knew. And the other kids know I knew. So it's not a total loss. I've just got to try to be faster next time and a bit more dramatic.

Aha! Fortune has changed! Robbie's gotten the answer wrong! My hand bolts skyward triumphantly. I'm back in action, baby!

You laugh. But if we're honest, many of us hold onto versions of this behavior well into adulthood. In me, this might surface as an insatiable need to send a follow-up email or text after I've noticed an error in the original I sent, simply for the purpose of letting the recipient know that I'm well aware of the word that was misspelled. This might be accompanied by some explanation of how I was in a hurry or slipped on the keyboard or was tired when I sent it. A little voice inside tells me that if I do not, they will certainly replace any prior thoughts that I'm an intelligent person with an irrevocable opinion that I am a dolt.

THE BEST ADVICE SO FAR:
It's not all that important for people to know that you know.

So you don't have the compulsion to correct errors in communications *ex post facto*. Maybe it's the relatively harmless but annoying habit of blurting answers during crowd games—even when you're on the other team.

Maybe it's interrupting others mid-story to be sure they know that you've been there, done that, or accomplished something just a touch more amazing than whatever they've just shared. I remember hearing a comedian once who ventured into religion and speculated about what it might have been like if Mary were one of these know-it-alls, joining in conversation with the other mothers of the village:

Other mother: "My little Nathaniel sat up today!"

Mary: "Well, I gave Jesus a bath this morning, and the little dear just crawled *right* up on top of the *water!*"

I suspect this is only funny because it involves Mary. In real life? Not so cute.

As will be discussed further in the upcoming chapter on loss, this can turn up in the tendency to draw attention to yourself when others are going through a difficult time: "Oh, I know! When this happened to *me* a couple of years back..." And off you go making sure they know that "you know exactly how they feel."

My friend Brandon got into a heated argument with his father, who had mentioned a certain actor in context of a movie—a movie in which my friend was sure said actor had not appeared. Mind you, the actual topic of conversation was not the movie. Rather, as I recall, Brandon's father had been trying to compliment him by comparing him to some noble quality or other illustrated by the movie in question. However, instead of being able to appreciate the compliment, the drive to point out the misinformation and let his dad know that he knew it was an error, resulted instead in full-out anger that lasted for several days.

Perhaps even more irritating is letting people know that you know—without ever saying a word. They're telling you what they think of a political stance or how they plan to handle a certain interpersonal situation, and you just smile in a way that says, "Oh, isn't that priceless that you *actually think* that, you poor, misinformed soul!"

I'm frequently struck with the idea that, somewhere in time, perhaps in the year 1128 A.D., there was a man who thought he knew a lot about a lot of things and went about expounding upon them often and with great urgency to his friends and neighbors and passersby. And he is dead now, buried in some unmarked place on a hill, or by the edge of some forest or other. Even his name is long forgotten, to say nothing of all that information and opinion he felt the world needed so desperately to hear during his time walking the planet. That is not meant to be a downer. It's simply a reminder that the world will go on just fine without knowing that we know.

I have to laugh as I imagine that childhood me at his desk, trying to apply this advice. The teacher has just asked the question, and he is sitting tight-lipped with fingers intertwined so tightly that his knuckles are turning white. Breathing is erratic and clammy sweat forms along his hairline in his effort to keep his hand down—to actually let the moment pass *without* letting the class know that he knows. At recess, he will certainly have more than a handful of casual conversations to explain to his playmates that he *did* know and was merely making strides to becoming a better person by exercising restraint and letting someone else have a turn.

Don't get me wrong. I'm not saying that we should never make ourselves heard or share information. I'm simply suggesting that we consider carefully *why* we feel we need to share it.

Will the information help someone in a practical way? Or is it more self serving?

Is it welcomed by the listener? Or thrust upon them, whether they like it or not?

Ask yourself, "Will there be any negative consequences if I do not let people know this right now?" And if no negative consequences can be identified, follow up with, "What positive effects will this have on others if I share it?"

Often, in social settings, the nature of the conversation is simply people sharing and enjoying the entertainment of stories well told. We all know that friend who gets people roaring with their over-the-top version of some event or other. Maybe that person is you. I've been known to spin a tale or two myself that has kept audiences locked in and wanting more. And sometimes, part of this social exchange is one-upping each other—delivering a spiral of stories that mount in outrageousness, all in good fun. Is this giving in to that need to let others know that you know? Well, I would ask, is my main point that I need the attention? Or is it truly to enhance the enjoyment of guests who like to hear a good adventure, which would certainly qualify as having a positive effect on others? If you start to feel that you *must* speak, or you feel a competitive or envious boil begin when others are getting the attention instead of you at the moment, you are likely fighting the former. If you find you are enjoying listening to the stories others are telling without the urge to break in and take over, you're probably on good ground.

When others sense that you are driven by that need to let them know what you know, their usual response is avoidance. No one likes a know-it-all. People may excuse themselves and not return to the conversation. Others may just begin to avoid social interaction with you altogether. Still others will become irritated and hyper focus on any verbal or factual error you may make, calling it out in front of others as a means of putting you in your place.

My friends Dib and Holly and I have a sort of assumed code of behavior when we are at parties together. We keep an eye on one another, and if we realize that one of the others has been cornered by someone driven by the need to expound at length upon what they know, we sidle over and politely interject with, "I'm sorry to interrupt, but when you get a moment, could I see you in the kitchen?" We affectionately call this "saving" one another.

Try being aware, and then be honest with yourself about what you notice. If you find these things happening around you, it may well be that you're still raising your figurative hand too much.

Questions for Reflection and Discussion:

APPENDIX page 335

CHAPTER 8

The Limelight: Sharing

I'M GOING TO BEGIN THIS CHAPTER where the last left off, giving one more example of someone who had a controlling need to make sure people knew that he knew. It involves a visit I made some years back to the home of a young man I mentored at the time. I'll present the scene in the form of a play, though I'll have to truncate some of it, so that I don't completely lose you to boredom during the numerous, long-winded monologues. I've interjected "notes to self" with my thoughts along the way.

In the previous chapter, I mentioned that there are those among us who enjoy telling wild tales for the sheer enjoyment of the listener. It's likewise a temptation for a writer to embellish stories, in order to better entertain the reader. Alas, that is not the case with the cautionary tale that follows. While I have changed some of the exact details to disguise identities, the nature and flow of this conversation is precisely the way it all went down:

[Erik rings the doorbell. The door opens. Father, Mother and 15-year-old Henry greet Erik. After greetings, Mother excuses herself to kitchen to finish dinner preparation. Father gestures to adjacent living room where he, Erik and Henry sit. Father seats himself in large, red, upholstered chair. Erik sits on full-sized sofa. Henry attempts to join Erik on sofa.]

Father: No, Henry, why don't you sit over there [gestures to small, decorative chair] so that our guest isn't crowded.

(note to self... *Crowded? With two people on a full-size sofa?*)

Erik [turning to smile at Henry]: Well, it's nice to come and see where you live, Henry. Thanks for inviting me.

Father: We've lived here since before Henry was even born. I remember when we first moved in. The things we were really looking for in a house were... (truncate portion of long-winded monologue)... and the upstairs had this little room that we figured [aside to Henry]—Stop slouching, Henry. Sit up—[continuing]... that we figured I could use as a den... (truncate portion of continued long-winded monologue).

(note to self... *How does this have anything to do with my telling Henry that it was nice to see where he lived and thanking him for inviting me? Does the Father actually believe that I am interested in this detailed account about the house itself, the number of closets, etc.?*)

Mother [peeking around corner]: Dinner should be ready in about 15 minutes, guys.

Erik [seizing the moment]: So, Henry, how was school today?

Henry [glancing nervously at Father, as if for permission to speak, then sheepishly]: Well… it was OK. A little stressful, but…

Father: Henry, stop mumbling. It's very hard for anyone to understand what you're saying when you mumble like that. And it's not stressful. It's just called hard work, if you're going to bring up those grades we talked about.

(note to self… *apparently, it wasn't all that difficult for anyone to understand clearly what Henry had said, since Father refers to it here.*)

Father [continuing, to Erik]: Henry's last grade report was a real disappointment. He had a C in Biology. He's perfectly capable of all As if he would apply himself. It's just laziness. Why, when I was in school [aside to Henry]—Don't do that with your fingers. It makes you look ridiculous and it's rude. It makes it seem like you aren't even interested in the guest you invited!—[continuing] Anyway, like I said, when I was in school, my father made us come right home and sit at the dining room table until all of our work was done. None of this sitting in your room or on the couch... (truncate portion of long-winded monologue about the way it was when Father was in school).

Things continued this way throughout the entire evening—with my trying to direct conversation to Henry, only to have his father quickly turn it back to himself, interspersed only with critical comments toward a silent Henry. During dinner and after, as we sat at the table a bit longer, Henry's mother just smiled and said nothing at all. Henry looked completely dejected, only able between his father's extended monologues to shoot me the occasional glance that at once said both "I'm sorry" and "I'm completely embarrassed."

I recently got into a discussion with this young man, who is now in his twenties. I asked how he thought he'd changed for the better in the last ten years. There were a few close friends around. Henry quirked his mouth to the side in a sort of awkward smile, his head lowered. His eyes darted around the room quickly, as if to see if anyone objected to his answering my question. Then he said, "Um... I think... I've gotten more self-confidence."

And he has! I see it in dozens of ways. But those years of having the limelight taken off of him for all things good — while being shined glaringly on every perceived fault — are still taking their toll on him, even a decade later.

THE BEST ADVICE SO FAR:
Make it your goal to foster others-centered moments as opposed to me-centered moments.

Please don't misunderstand my sharing that anecdote to be some outcry against Henry's father. He's a likable guy in many ways. My point is that spotlight stealing does not contribute to healthy relationships or happy people.

If you struggle with that itch, as I did, to be heard—to let people know that you know—the answer is not simply to sit quietly and bite your tongue whenever others are present. While that may sometimes be *exactly* the right thing for you to do, there is also the wonderful possibility of using "what you know" to become an expert at noticing others' reactions and directing positive attention toward them.

Before offering some suggestions for turning the spotlight onto others, I want to point out that the goal here is not to avoid talking about yourself at all costs. If you never share meaningful information about yourself, you will likely be perceived as evasive, ingratiating or self-righteous. The trick is to know when and how much to share. I have found that, if you turn the spotlight to others, they turn it back onto you in a natural way. I presented some self-screening questions in the last chapter that may help in determining your motivations. In short, if you feel a *drive* or *need* to speak about yourself, you likely have things out of balance.

So how can we actively trade some of those me-centered moments for others-centered ones? I'll offer some tried-and-true approaches that I use often. But once you get a taste for the joy it brings, your own creativity will likely come up with countless other ways to bring positive attention to the people around you.

Compliment

It's somewhat alarming to me how many social kindnesses are rapidly going the way of the dodo. But the effect of a simple and sincere compliment is still as profound as ever. If you've gotten out of practice, getting ready to give a compliment may very well make the back of your neck go all tingly. Take that as an indicator of the positive power in what you are about to do. (And isn't it wonderful how alive that *zing* makes you feel?)

Here are some keys to giving a compliment with class and maximum effectiveness:

A compliment should be sincere. To compliment on something that you're not convinced is really all that terrific, just for the sake of "saying something nice," usually just winds up feeling awkward for both parties. Also, avoid the common pitfall of giving what I call "backhanded compliments"—compliments with a qualifier tacked on due to nerves, wit, mixed motives or insincerity. A couple of examples are "You're pretty smart... for a girl" or "You're really fun to hang around with, when I actually ever hear from you."

A compliment should be given solely as a gift to the receiver, and not in hopes of getting something in return. This means that slurring "Hey, baby, how'd you get your bad self in them jeans?" at the club doesn't really count for our purposes.

While complimenting someone on an article of clothing or a haircut is all well and good, the best compliments are those that reflect character and action:

"You have a great smile."

"I think it's amazing how much you care about other people."

"I admire the way you let that older man go first in line."

The more of those tingly sensations you get as you prepare to deliver a compliment, the more likely you are getting at something real about the person.

The best compliments are specific. "You're really awesome" would be even better as "You really cheered me up today when I was feeling down. You do that a lot for people!"

A compliment is a gift of time and focus as much as it is a gift of words. Always make eye contact when giving a compliment in person. And, if you know it, use the person's name. Eye contact and hearing one's name have a way of causing heartfelt words to sink in even deeper. Of course, not every compliment must be given in person. I'm a big fan of texting compliments throughout the day, sending short emails that have no purpose other than the compliment, and, yes... sending those outdated thingies called letters and cards. You'd be surprised how special someone feels when they know you took the time to hand write a note or card and drop it off at the post office.

Thank

Expressing thanks is very similar to giving a compliment and, in most ways, can follow the same principles. Sometimes, the lines even blur. But saying thank you tends to be an even more personal way of pointing out the many praiseworthy qualities in others.

I like to thank and appreciate people often. In addition to thanking people face to face, I employ a variety of media, including voice mail, texts, emails, and social network messaging. This is a wonderful use of the technology made available to us. In addition, I still hold to the idea that hand-written thanks is still very much worth doing. It communicates something different. Something—*more.* It's as if a piece of the writer is captured in the written word. When I see personal handwriting, I feel the person in it.

He took time to sit and pen this.

She touched this paper.

She formed these loops and lines with part of herself.

He put his heart into this.

This is special.

It's about more than social etiquette and showing

appreciation, however. Investing time and thought into expressing our thanks changes us, as well.

Late last year, a young friend of mine confessed that he'd been struggling with depression. He just couldn't seem to shake it, and he asked for my advice. I suggested that he take the next 30 days and write a thank-you letter or card to one person every day. Some of them, he could mail or deliver. But some might even be written to people from the past with whom he'd fallen out of contact. He seemed confused as to how this would in any way help him with his doldrums. I explained that the task wasn't so much aimed at those to whom the letters would be written, but rather at changing his own perspective.

He balked at first, certain that he did not even know that many people, much less people he could thank. But I gently assured him that, if he put his mind to it, he could do it. I encouraged him not to look at the 30 days as a whole, but to simply think about whom he might write to first.

A few days later, I spoke with him again. He had taken my suggestion seriously. And something had happened.

He explained with excitement how he had written the first one to someone, and that this had made him think of another person he wanted to write to. In writing to the second person, he thought of another whole *category* of people he hadn't really considered before then, of people he really would like to thank. Somewhere in the process of thinking about thankfulness—he became more thankful. And in spending the time to remember and write out all of the thank-worthy things people in his life had done for him, he no longer found himself feeling depressed.

Thankfulness begets more thankfulness. A lack thereof turns the spotlight back onto ourselves, leaving us focused on what seems wrong with our lives instead of what is right.

Ask

There's an old line of humor, poking fun at the classic narcissistic socialite attempting to be others-focused: "Oh, *stop*! *Really*, darling, enough about *me*. Let's talk about *you*! So then... what do *you* think of my fabulous new dress?"

The humor here lies in the irony, because, in reality, asking questions about others is a near sure-fire way to keep the spotlight on them and not yourself.

Let that sink in. If you can master the art of asking rather than telling, you will have virtually guaranteed that you will avoid the pitfalls of being an attention hog. What's more, you will become known as a genuine and caring listener, because truly listening is foundational to asking meaningful, others-centered questions. In fact, this is even a cornerstone practice of successful counseling.

Consider the following exchanges, the first illustrating telling and the second, asking.

Conversation #1:

Tim: What a terrible day at work!

John: Seems to be going around. My friend Sam just quit his job last week. He'd been there five years. Must've really hated it.

Tim: Wow, that sounds tempting right about now.

John: I don't love my job, but I don't hate it. And it pays the bills.

Tim: Well, you're lucky then.

John: Yeah, I guess I am. And [spotlight has shifted to John]…

Conversation #2:

Tim: What a terrible day at work!
John: Oh, man, what happened?

Tim: My boss was just on a rampage. It was like, no matter what I did, she wasn't happy.

John: Is she usually like that?

Tim: No, I guess not. There must be something going on with her.

John: That's too bad. I hope she works it out soon, for everyone's sake! Well, for now, work's over. Do you have anything fun planned for tonight?

Tim: Nah, TV then bed.

John: Are you into a particular show? Or do you watch just to have something on?

Tim: Well, don't laugh [he laughs] but… I'm totally into that show *Bimbo Alley*. Don't tell anyone!

The trick is to listen intently to what the other person is saying and ask questions that focus on what *they* have said, instead of thinking about what *you* would like to say next or just inserting an unrelated question:

Tim: What a terrible day at work!

John: So… what do you think about last Saturday's football game?

While this may wind up actually working as a diversion, it doesn't have quite the same effect as careful listening resulting in thoughtful questions.

Of course, once your questions have helped Tim find something to get his mind off work, if you happen to share his affinity for trash TV, feel free to tell him that you love *Bimbo Alley*, as well. Constant questioning can grow tiresome or annoying if it is just for the sake of asking, rather than really focusing on the person. Talking about common interests, on the other hand, is spotlight *sharing*, which is a terrific and balanced way to build relationships.

One last thought on asking questions. If the intention to be others-centered isn't kept at the forefront, questions can actually wind up perpetuating me-centered conversation just as easily as anything else. I know many people who are all too happy to keep me *talking* while really keeping the attention on themselves and their own needs. For example, "You always have good advice. What do you think I should do about my girlfriend wanting to hang out with other guys?" Here, we see both a compliment and a question in play. But while this may be a perfectly legitimate question for the appropriate time and place, make no mistake that it is me-centered and not others-centered. Know the difference. Don't trick yourself into thinking you're being others-centered just because you happen to have asked a question. If your purpose is to turn the spotlight on someone else, keep the questions focused on them and not "what they think of your dress."

Reflect

This is another valuable "technique" for keeping the spotlight on others. Similar to a mirror's reflection, verbal reflection is simply repeating a key word or phrase back to the speaker, or stating what you notice. Like focused questioning, reflection is another tool used in effective counseling. But it is certainly not restricted to therapy. It works in all communication settings, because it shows that you are interested and engaged, while gently encouraging the speaker to elaborate. Let's pick up with Tim and John.

Tim: What a terrible day at work!

John: *Terrible?*

Tim: Well, maybe not terrible, but everyone was on my case about the smallest things.

John: *Everyone* was on your case.

Tim: Not literally "everyone." It felt like everyone, but I guess it was mainly just my supervisor and this girl Kate who's handling the media end of my project.

John: Well, whether it was everyone or just a couple of people, it really seems to have affected you today.

Careful and thoughtful reflection is another virtually fail-safe way to keep the focus on someone else rather than turning it onto yourself. More on reflection in an upcoming chapter.

Invite

Inviting in this sense is simply opening a door for someone to talk. In a group setting, this might be as simple as turning to someone who hasn't said anything recently and saying, "Hey, Mike, you've been awfully quiet tonight. What's on your mind?" More often, it is creating opportunities for others to be seen in a positive light.

Whereas me-centered motivation grasps for openings in conversation where I can be the center of attention and look better, invitation allows these openings to pass to someone else who may not take them otherwise. Here are some examples (assuming that George, Becky or Luke are in present company, respectively):

"Hey, George, why don't you tell everyone about your new job."

"Everyone, you have to hear what happened to Becky yesterday! It's pretty cool!"

"Did you guys know that Luke can sing? I heard him in the car yesterday and was blown away!"

Now, again, there's nothing wrong with taking moments to tell about *your own* new job, amazing adventure, and the like. There's a time and a place for everything. But in situations when you are already in the limelight, it's a tribute to solid character, as well as a wonderful gift, to be willing to graciously turn the stage over to someone else.

So, you've told about your own trip to Europe and everyone is mesmerized. You could bask in the attention all evening if you like, telling enthralling tale after tale of your exploits, even keeping everybody quite interested and entertained. But imagine, after you've had the floor for a bit, saying, "Yeah, traveling is unbelievable. Actually, did you guys all know that Dan spent a few months traveling in South America when he was in college? Tell them about that family you stayed with in Ecuador, Dan." Dan is a figment of my imagination, and I *still* smile at the thought of seeing my other imaginary friends all turn to Dan with anticipation.

I was discussing these ideas with my friend Chad, midway through writing this chapter. He made a good observation, one worthy of including here. People who are driven to steal the limelight are generally motivated by the desire to have others like them, to think they are unique, interesting and cool. Sadly, creating me-centered moments nearly always has the opposite effect, causing others to avoid us and form negative opinions. However, those who take the time to become adept at creating others-centered moments stand out, are sought-after company, and earn an all-around positive reputation. What's more, when you learn to turn the spotlight on others, it actually brings with it a higher level of personal happiness than keeping it all for yourself.

Questions for Reflection and Discussion:

APPENDIX page 337

CHAPTER 9

Names

CHOOSING A NAME FOR A BABY is no mean feat. In fact, today it's got its own market. Considerations include the meaning of a name, its country of origin, how it sounds with a certain middle name, whether a beloved family member past or present held the name, which famous (or infamous) people may have shared the name, and what possible nicknames (both kind and unkind) may be. Even how easy the name will be to learn to spell in Kindergarten, or how it will look on a future business card, are included in the process. It's a wonder anyone winds up with a name at all.

Then there are the sensationalistic stories, where someone tries to name their baby a naughty or controversial word as some expression of their freedom of speech. Or they try to get away with using "Π^2/Picasso" as a name, in order to seem edgy and *avant garde*.

As adults, some just find their name unappealing, and go to court to trade "Lucy" for "Sunshine," or "Mehitabel" for the more unassuming "Mary."

Once names are assigned or chosen, they become commodities, exchanged or denied in their own sort of economy. We marry and change last names. Or hyphenate them. Or don't take a spouse's new name at all. Some choose to drop a last name in favor of resuming a former name upon divorce, or to dissociate from parents. Still others adopt an entirely new name upon blending established families.

Those parents who labored in love to find just the right combination for their little one's name later use it to strike fear into misbehaving children: "*Jonathan Percival Carter*, you leave your sister alone *this instant*!" I'm unsure as to whether this occurs as a reminder of original ownership rights, or as a means of filling the mouth long enough not to swear.

Then, of course, titles and nicknames and pet names get thrown into the mix, and you'd darn-well better know which combination to choose depending on relationship, setting, and intangible emotional factors. A female child named Jane Frances Smith may be called many things in her lifetime.

She is simply "Jane" to her girlfriends in grade school, but perhaps "Janie Brainy" to the taunting boys.

However, when she receives her Ph.D. in astrophysics, her closest friends rarely call her "Jane" anymore, but rather have re-adopted "Janie Brainy" or just "Brainy," which is now a term of endearment. Her TA calls her "Jane" in private, but "Doctor Smith" at school functions or in front of students. The students call her "Doctor Smith," as well, except those few whom she has invited to call her "Doc."

Her sister still calls her "Jan-Fran," but she is the only one allowed to do so.

Mom calls her "Janie" or "Baby Doll," the latter of which her husband tried to get away with calling her once and was met with a warning glare stern enough to end that particular pet name. He calls her "Janie" or "Sweetheart." Sometimes late at night, he calls her "Doctor" in a low and sultry tone of voice, but that is certainly none of our business.

Her daughter calls her "Mom" and her son calls her "Ma." That is, of course, unless they need to butter her up for something, in which case they call her "Mumsy" or "Mumsicle." When they really want to tick her off, they call her "Jane." When they no longer value their freedom or their lives, they brave "Frances."

Her nieces and nephews called her "Auntie Jane" when they were younger, but have taken to calling her "Aunt Jane" in recent years, much to her dismay. Whenever they do so, she cuts them off with "…that's Auntie Jane, please."

The children at church call her "Mrs. Smith," or, as they get to know her, "Miss Janie."

And this is all over a girl named "Jane Smith," no less.

Imagine how confusing it might all have gotten had she been named "Elizabeth." The childhood taunt of "Janie Brainy" might have become "Booksy Betsy," but now we'd have to contend with "Lisa, Liza, Liz, Betty, Betsy, Beth," and a host of others. One reference I found listed nearly 100 possible nicknames for "Elizabeth."

In the end, what does it matter? It's just an arbitrary label, isn't it?

All of the hullabaloo over it would seem to suggest otherwise.

THE BEST ADVICE SO FAR:
Put the power and beauty of a name to good use.

A name is not just a word. It is an identity. Many have heard our name through flesh and amniotic fluid since before we were born. It is comfort. Whether spoken in love, lust, respect or anger, it says, "I see you" rather than "I see past you." It is an acknowledgment that we *are*.

I've noticed that when someone calls *me* "Erik," it sounds different to me than when they talk to or about another person by the same name. A name is infused with—*something*—when we speak it with intention to its owner.

Why is it, then, that we go about life ignoring the names of most people around us, denying each other of that important piece of our central identity?

"But I don't know those people's names," you may protest. True. And it would be impossible to know the name of every passer-by. But for hundreds of people around us daily, it *is* possible to break the cycle of isolation that we tend to fall into, and to connect with others by knowing—and *using*—their names.

Let's start easy. Most service workers wear a name tag:

The drive-thru worker at the coffee shop.

The pool maintenance man.

The receptionist at the doctor's office.

The bank teller.

The *maître d'*, wait staff, bartenders and bussers at restaurants.

The cashiers, baggers and runners at the grocery store.

The guy who works in the electronics department at WalMart.

Such name tags are all around us. And for what purpose do you imagine that they exist? Someone somewhere thought it might be a good customer service *relations* move. But if we are completely honest, if we acknowledge the names of these people (*people, PEOPLE!*) at all, it is when we are dissatisfied with their performance or have some other bone to pick with the establishment. How terrible it must be, to only hear your name spoken in anger and irritation, eight or more hours a day, five days a week.

But imagine simply saying, "Hi, Charlene, how's your day going?" to that teller. Or "Thank you, Mark. You've been a big help" to the kid who helped you with your bags at the grocer.

I'm going to go out on a limb and make a bold claim here. That is, ignoring names in such everyday cases is an indicator that we are treating people as *props*—machines that exist solely for our comfort and benefit—rather than as the human beings they are. Conversely, when I notice and use someone's name, I am treating them as I would like to be treated — with care and kindness, as a real person.

What's more, I can usually offer *my own* name.

It's simple really, though it may take a jump start for you to get into the habit. So imagine. I'm at a restaurant. My server comes over and says, "Hi, my name is Julian and I'll be your server. Can I start you off with something to drink today?" (Note: the interaction thus far is scripted, and does not constitute "real communication" merely because Julian has provided his name.) I reply, "Hi, Julian, my name is Erik. Nice to meet you. Yes, I think I'll have a Diet Coke, thanks." Aha! Now, the invisible wall has been shattered. I've used his name and given my own. Small niceties were included, but real *connection* with another human being has happened, because of my choice to use our names. And I can all but guarantee that Julian's next reply will *not* continue on-script with, "One Diet Coke. I'll be right back to take your order."

Was this difficult? For some, it might be a slight challenge. But the mechanics of it are certainly not hard to handle.

So, what about all those people who don't go around making it easy for us by wearing name tags? News flash: they've invented this handy new strategy called… *asking*.

Let's go back to the restaurant. My server is not wearing a name tag. He says, "Hi, can I start you off with something to drink today?" I reply, "Hi, I'm Erik. What's your name?" He says, "Oh, hi, Erik. I'm Julian."

It's almost magical, I tell you. Works every time.

I have a heart for the homeless. Shaking their cups and cans for money doesn't really bother me. But I've found, from Providence to Paris, that a bigger gift than money is asking someone's name, telling them mine, and then talking with them for a moment or two, using their name often.

I recall asking one such homeless woman for her name. She hesitated. She couldn't remember. She'd been called many things over the years, but it had been so long since she'd heard her own name spoken that she'd nearly forgotten it. Speaking someone's name gives them dignity. Equality. It restores their humanity, if only for those moments.

Moving around your day with the intention of interacting—knowing people and being known—changes everything. It results in more smiles. More surprises. More reminders that you are alive and on a planet with billions of other unique and fascinating individuals.

I'd just gotten back from my second trip to North Carolina within a two-week stretch. Road trips do you in. You eat junk food from whichever chain restaurants and convenience stores present the fastest off-and-on to the highway. In this case, I'd done so for sixteen hours. Leaves you feeling not so fresh and sunny the next day. So, for lunch the next day, I stopped at a sit-down restaurant and ordered just a Diet Coke and a salad.

Despite my paltry order and its promise of a pittance of a tip, my server, Marcella, treated me as if I were a party of four ordering up a storm. She was friendly and accommodating, and checked on me often.

While I waited, I noticed a particular bus boy, a tall kid with glasses who smiled even when it appeared that no one was looking. I watched him as he looked for people to help. As servers came by with empties, he would step out and say, "Let me take that for you." If someone ran out of bread, he offered to refill it. When I removed my straw wrapper and placed it off to the side of the table, he came over with a smile: "Let me get that." He was not wearing a name tag. I asked Marcella. She said his name was Brandon, and that he was new. I told her how remarkable I'd found him, how he stood out for his pleasant nature and work ethic.

I then asked another server passing by if she might get the manager for me. The manager was a smartly-dressed young man named Shawn. I told him that I wanted to "reverse complain" about Marcella and Brandon. He smiled broadly, not sure if this was a joke. I told him how much I had appreciated Marcella's service and attentiveness, in spite of my small order. I told him all I had noticed about the hard-working Brandon, adding, "You'd better keep *that* one around!"

Shawn shook his head. "That's really cool! When people call for me, it's nearly always to complain. You have no idea how infrequently we hear what we are doing *right*." We shook hands and off he went.

When Marcella returned, she told me that Shawn had given me my lunch on the house. This was entirely unnecessary, but much appreciated. I tipped Marcella anyway, and left.

Once home, I looked up the address for the restaurant. I took note of Shawn's last name, which was posted online. This took all of one minute. I then wrote a quick thank-you card for his kindness, expressing what an enjoyable lunch I'd had all around, and popped it in the mail. This was *not* my way of hoping for another free lunch. It was just taking some time and simple measures to treat people as people—to live *with* them, instead of merely living *around* them.

I shared this story with my friend Chad and told him that

I might write about it. He thought it was very cool, indeed, but wondered if some people might be disappointed when they try to repeat the experiment, and *don't* wind up with free lunch or some other personal benefit as a result. My thought to him was that, if you are engaging with people for what you can get out of it, that is manipulation. And manipulation doesn't always work. But if you are doing it because you want to value people and have genuine interactions with them, you will always come out of it feeling rewarded.

Using people's names is just one more way to stay outward focused, instead of being all about me. Whether it is your neighbors, co-workers, gas attendants or people on the train, each has a real life. An important life. Struggles. Goals. Dreams. Families. At core, I believe we each want to connect. To matter.

We each have a name. Look for opportunities to really *see* people. Interact. Be vulnerable. Be genuine. Before long, what may have once seemed daunting will become a natural, full and enjoyable way of life.

Questions for Reflection and Discussion:

APPENDIX page 339

CHAPTER 10

Kindness

IN THE EARLY 1990s, the term "Random Acts of Kindness" was all the rage when a book by the same name was released. Everyone was abuzz about it, as if this were the first time anyone had thought to be nice to anyone and—gasp!—for *no apparent reason*! As I recall, the challenge was also to try to remain anonymous, so that you weren't doing it just for the rush of being thanked.

I considered myself a pretty nice guy, but even I was inspired. I was just thinking about it more, I guess. Looking for opportunities to jump on the RAK bandwagon. I remember being at an amusement park, in a line for food behind two teenage girls. They were trying to figure out how both of them could eat on four dollars and change— no mean feat at amusement park prices. I had a little extra money, so I pulled out a ten, folded it until it fit in my palm, and tapped one of the girls on the shoulder. "Here," I said, holding out my downturned fist. She looked at me as if I were going to drop a scorpion in her hand. I flicked the folded bill into my fingertips like a magic trick and added, "Get something to eat." They took it, still a little spooked. I walked away (it was the closest I could come to remaining anonymous under the circumstances). As I was leaving, I heard them excitedly chattering about what they could now eat. It felt good.

Some years later, Random Acts of Kindness got a facelift with the "Pay It Forward" movement. Another book was behind the push, followed by a movie where we got to see the creepy "I see dead people" kid in a less creepy role. Unless you count ending the movie with the kid getting shot in a Random Act of Violence as creepy. No one could blame you.

The twist with Paying It Forward was that you were supposed to do the nice thing with the understanding that the next person had to do something nice for someone else, and so on and so on.

Within a year, in 2001, the Twin Towers were attacked. It rocked America to the core. And, once again, people remembered to be kind to one another. Neighbors who hadn't ever introduced themselves stood side by side along streets, holding candles and talking about things that mattered.

That was all so long ago. Ah, the droll days of yester-year, when kindness was cool.

Wait.

Hasn't it always been cool? Isn't it *still* kind of cool?

THE BEST ADVICE SO FAR:
Kindness still works.

We get in this mindset that, if Oprah is talking about it, we just have to try it. But next month, it will be the new no-diet-no-exercise weight-loss pill. Or taking your dog to some guy who whispers to it.

But kindness is not a fad. It's a choice. It's a mindset. It's a lifestyle.

"Yes," you protest, "but all the good acts of kindness, like paying for the person behind you in the drive-thru or at the toll booth, have been done to death."

And I reply with a hearty, "So?" Can kindness really be overdone? I've heard of killing someone with kindness, but I hadn't considered it an actual threat.

I still try to make Random Acts of Kindness a regular practice. It is not a *duty*, mind you. It's fun. I like it. It energizes me.

So, I'm driving through at the local coffee shop, and I say, "I'm feeling a random act of kindness right now. Please ring in the order of the person behind me along with mine." The teller smiles and is perhaps inspired to look for her own opportunities. But for now, I share the fun of the experience at hand by letting her deliver the news. And I can assure you that whoever gets to the window next is not thinking, "Oh brother. That is *so* 1995." I love to do this and then just *imagine* the response. As I play it out, the woman has had a long, hard day and felt unappreciated. She gets the news that her coffee is on the house, courtesy of a stranger. She smiles broadly and is reminded of what is right with the world instead of wrong. She puts on her radio and, as luck would have it, her favorite song from her youth is just starting to play.

Hey, it could happen. The point is, I enjoy the possibilities. It causes me to have a brighter outlook and an impish sort of Christmas spirit all year long.

Chad, who attended Penn State, started an organization called The Clown Nose Club. (Don't wince; it has nothing to do with actual clowns.) Their philosophy and mission are written specifically, but the *For Dummies* version goes something like this: "to go out of your way to let people know they matter." That's it? That's the stated goal of a whole club? Yes. Yes, it is. And you would not believe the response. No sooner had this club started than stories were hitting the newspaper, and radio shows were asking my friend to talk about it to their listeners. In its fledgling months in existence, the club drew more than 80 members.

They say that bad news sells. I'm here to tell you that good news and happiness sell, too. People can't get enough of a *good* thing. Kindness doesn't go out of style. Truth is, kindness not only helps others, it improves your own outlook on life. And that just makes the world a better place.

Questions for Reflection and Discussion:

APPENDIX page 341

CHAPTER 11

Rules of Engagement

WHENEVER I STEP into a new mentoring relationship, I immediately set "ground rules." I've found that setting these up from the very beginning creates an immediate sense of security and a healthy dose of anticipation. Here's how the honesty portion of these ground rules might sound:

"There are three things that are very important to me when I decide to start a new relationship. First, we have to agree to be completely honest. If we don't have honesty, we don't have a foundation for anything else. Honesty doesn't mean you have to tell me everything. It just means that what you *do* choose to tell me is the truth. So if I ask you about something, you could say, 'I don't really want to talk about that right now,' and that is still being honest, because it is the truth. Second, we have to agree to confidentiality. That means that we agree to keep what we talk about between just us. I will keep anything you tell me to myself, unless I feel strongly that you are going to hurt yourself or someone else. And last, we have to agree to accept each other, no matter what. That means even if you get mad at me or I don't like something you decide to do, we are deciding right now that we will work it out."

These are both a challenge and a promise. I can't think

of a time in the last twenty years when this conversation met with anything but a positive reaction, or when a kid didn't take it very seriously.

With these things firmly in place, we are always coming from a point of strength. For instance, when I know there is a potentially difficult discussion ahead, I can start with, "We've promised to be honest with each other, right? So, I am thinking about some things that I need to be honest with you about, and I know you will be honest with me, too. Remember that whatever you tell me, I will keep to myself; and no matter what either of us says, we already know that we agreed to accept one another. So it will be fine."

These "rules" aren't somehow specific to a mentoring relationship. They apply to all personal relationships. So in my adult friendships, though the tone of the ground-rules conversation may be different, the content is the same:

"I feel like we've moved beyond being acquaintances to being real friends now; so, for me, when I make that choice to really be friends, it means I'm committing to honesty and confidentiality at all times. And I take friendship seriously, so once I decide to cross that line into friendship, you're stuck with me." This is usually followed by a great discussion that we refer to often. Having positive expectations in place—a pact of sorts—is an anchor that keeps a relationship grounded, solid.

THE BEST ADVICE SO FAR:
Set clearly-stated, positive expectations for your relationships.

There has been substantial buzz in the last couple of decades over establishing boundaries in relationships. It seems a shame to me that there is so much to say about the importance of drawing lines with people, and so comparatively little to say about erasing them. About setting positive expectations regarding how to engage with others on a deeper, more meaningful level.

Maybe you're thinking of some relationships you have where you didn't start out with this kind of expectations, and you wish you had. Good news. Setting these ground rules early on is fantastic; but having a heartfelt discussion with the goal of setting positive expectations at *any* point in a relationship works just as well. It can even create a new beginning, of sorts—a landmark for change.

Once these "ground rules" are in place, don't let difficult or dodgy situations be the only reminders! Make them a comfortable part of your relationship and refer to them often (e.g., "I'm glad we're always honest with each other. It makes life so much easier that I can just be myself around you.").

Questions for Reflection and Discussion:

APPENDIX page 343

CHAPTER 12

Honesty

IF YOU'VE CHOSEN TO READ THIS BOOK THROUGH from cover to cover, you noted in the previous chapter the benefits of setting clear expectations in a relationship, including the bit where you agree to be honest at all times. If you are reading this chapter while tired, impaired by medication, or otherwise not on top of your game—beware! You may wind up being confused. Why? Because I'm about to tell you not to be honest.

A decade or more back, I had a conversation with my best friend, Dib, in which I was fighting to the death to defend my stand that, in relationships, the utmost honesty is always the best policy. I can see Dib's face even now. She's completely incredulous. I may as well have been a teenager telling my best friend that I was sure that kissing too long makes babies. "You *really* believe that? Oh boy, are you in for trouble."

I considered her a reasonable, intelligent, kind person with good relationships. How could she defend the idea that honesty is *not* always the best policy? I was reeling with the impending inevitability that I would hereafter be forced to number my best friend among the other Big Fat Liars of the world.

She has not changed her position. I'm happy to report that she is still my best friend. She is not, moreover, a Big Fat Liar. The simple truth is that she was right.

I'm so convinced of this, in fact, that it has been a staple of advice which I've passed along to countless others since.

THE BEST ADVICE SO FAR:
Honesty is not always the best policy.

Well, where does that leave me concerning my seemingly contradictory advice? How can I recommend that honesty be a ground rule of your relationships, and then add "but not always."

Some explanation is in order here.

You may recall from the last chapter that, as I see it, honesty does not mean complete divulgence. Honesty is not grounds to corner someone into having to tell you everything. I think sometimes people feel that if someone is not ready, able or willing to spill their guts at all times, it's a blow to trust and something must be wrong with the relationship. This is hardly the case. In fact, pushing for this to somehow *be* the case usually has a negative effect on relationships, causing others to feel annoyed, disrespected and smothered.

Similarly, honesty does not mean being tactlessly direct. Forthright. Aw, let's dispense with the pretty synonyms and call it what it is. Blunt. Rude. Hurtful.

To accept without discernment that "honesty is the best policy" is to give one's self a cart blanche license to be unkind, all the while claiming some moral high ground. This kind of "honesty" is without question *not* the best policy. On the contrary, it is a decidedly bad policy. And that is the gist of this bit of advice. In the running to have been the central piece of advice for this chapter was the idea that it is more important to be *kind* than to be right.

Revisit the erstwhile conversation I had with my friend, as she presents a case in point:

"So, if your wife asks, 'Does this dress make me look fat?' and you think it does, you would say so?"

"Well… yes." I reply. "Marriage is a relationship of trust, and trust means honesty at all times. So, even if it is a hard truth, I would say that telling her is the right thing to do."

She laughs aloud, shaking her head, and repeats her previous warning: "Boy oh boy, are you in for misery."

What an idiot I was.

Now in this theoretical example, I truly wasn't approaching it from a standpoint of justifying some desire to be rude. Or right. I really believed at that time in my life that direct honesty was a marker for all loving, healthy relationships.

Since then, I'm thrilled to say I've learned a few things. Among them is the fact that you can still be honest without being *brutally* honest. Pair this with a better understanding that *why* is more important than *what*, and you have a much better approach to relationships. *Why* is my wife asking if the dress makes her look fat? Is she feeling uncomfortable in the dress? Is she wanting affirmation that she is pretty? Is she worried that she's worn that dress too many times to events attended by the same people? Is she looking for grounds to shop and buy a new dress?

So, she asks if the dress makes her look fat. You've got to answer. The younger, ill-informed me might have replied, "Well, honey, if you want me to be honest, it does look a little tight around the midsection." I suspect that the younger, ill-informed me would have grown pretty comfortable with sleeping in the living room.

Some examples of what I might say now, reflecting truthfulness tempered with wisdom:

"If you're asking me that, it means *you* don't feel great in it. And I want you to feel great."

"You've had that dress a long time. Let's splurge and both get something new that we love."

"You could wear anything and still be beautiful to me, so you're asking the wrong person. I'm biased."

"Let's see what it looks like on. Then off. I'll tell you which I prefer." :: wink, wink::

The possibilities are endless. I'm not diverting the question here. I'm looking deeper into it. I'm listening to the heart and not just the words. And I have not been dishonest or deceptive in any way. I've just decided that kindness is a better guide than honesty at all costs.

Don't feel you are insightful enough to see the reason behind someone's asking a difficult question? Don't panic. Don't rush. As a failsafe, try this: "I'm more concerned about (or interested in) why you are asking me that."

In addition, consider using this checklist when deciding

if what you want to say needs to be said:

Is it true?

Is it kind?

Is it necessary?

Think of your interactions in the last day or so. Using this screening process, what *wouldn't* you have said? What grief could you have spared yourself and someone else? What positive, affirming things could you have said instead, that might have resulted in warm fuzzies rather than the cold shoulder?

Adopting a kindness-first approach to communication cannot help but lead to happier, healthier relationships.

Questions for Reflection and Discussion:

APPENDIX page 345

CHAPTER 13

Conversation

S O MAYBE you're feeling challenged lately to be a better listener—shining the spotlight a bit more on others and a bit less on yourself. Great! But what do you do when other people just aren't the talkative type?

:: cue the crickets ::

Certainly *that* is the right time to fill the empty space with your own words, right? You can. Or, you could try out some spiffy, new communication skills that might just come in handy.

THE BEST ADVICE SO FAR:
Learn to listen as well as you speak.

Becoming an effective communicator is an art form. As such, it takes time, patience and lots of practice. And it is never really perfected. But there are general principles that will help you draw others out while helping you tune in.

Ask Questions

As mentioned previously, knowing how to ask the right kind of questions is one of the most important interpersonal skills you can have. Here are a couple of guidelines for asking great questions:

<u>1. Ask *open* questions as opposed to *closed* questions.</u>

A *closed* question is one that has a limited set of possible responses. A few examples of *closed* questions:

"What's your name?"

"Have you eaten here before?"

"How's your meal?"

The first of these has essentially one answer with two varieties (the person's first name, or first and last). The second invites essentially two possible answers (*yes* or *no*). And the last also has a limited set of expected replies (*good, not good* and *so-so*).

"How are you doing today?" may also wind up being a *closed* question, since typical acceptable answers basically hail from the same set as the previous question.

Closed questioning is fine with communication partners who are inclined to share more information on their own. But with the reticent type, questions like these leave you back in silence after a word or two.

An *open* question is phrased to naturally require more from the response:

"What are your favorite things about summer?"

"How did you become interested in photography / motocross / design?"

"What's your week ahead looking like?"

The answers to these questions could be nearly anything. It's possible that *any* question can be greeted with "I don't know" or "same old same old"; but we'll address handling this type of response a little later.

By the way, for communication purposes, a *question* need not end in a question mark, but can also be a polite request for information: "So, tell me more about your job / semester / family."

One of my favorite *open* questions of this type is "Tell me three things you like about yourself." I usually follow this with, "…and then I'll tell you three things *I* like about you. But you have to tell me yours first."

2. Use *extension* questions.

Where it fits, the addition of "…and why" can help turn a *closed* question into an *open* one, or extend an open question even further. For example, "What's your favorite movie?" requires only a short answer, while "What's your favorite movie, and why?" invites a bit more insight:

"What was your favorite class this semester, *and why* did you like it so much?"

"If you could go anywhere in the world right now, all expenses paid, where would you go, *and why?*"

Other *extension* questions are basically re-phrasings of "Tell me more":

"I heard you won an award this week. *What's that all about?*"

"I saw a dent on your car. *How'd that happen?*"

"So, you've got a new job. *How's that going?*"

Observe Out Loud

A good deal of being an effective communicator is learning to be in the moment rather than letting your thoughts drift, and then truly focusing on the other person rather than on yourself. If you are worried about how your hair looks, or silently pondering the Discovery show you saw about how ostrich kicks can be deadly, you are not likely to connect deeply in current conversation.

A great strategy for keeping yourself in the moment, and for encouraging more input from your communication partner, is to actively observe and comment out loud on what you are noticing about them.

Recently, I was giving a voice lesson to a teen boy. I opened the lesson by previewing what we would be working on that day. Meanwhile, I jotted notes for him in his voice journal, which was on the piano in front of us. He seemed very focused on me indeed, as I spoke and wrote. When I finished my explanation, I turned to him. "OK, so do you understand our goals for today?"

He paused, and then replied with wide-eyed sincerity, "You have *really* clean ears!"

Now, while he *was* being observant, I'm not sure this is quite where we want to go with things. Aside from being somewhat awkward, albeit in an endearing fashion, this observation didn't lead anywhere. The best I could have said is, "Er… thanks." (In fact, I burst out laughing, as did he, and for quite some time.)

Instead, think of it this way. A good observation to share is one to which you could reasonably append "Tell me more."

Let's put my young friend's comment about the fastidiousness of my ear hygiene to the test:

"You have *really* clean ears! Tell me more."

Doesn't quite work, does it.
But, consider something more like this:

"That's a pretty nasty black eye."

"You're unusually quiet tonight."

"You aren't wearing your glasses."

"You made an interesting face when I mentioned your mom."

"You seem like you're in a really good space today."

In each case here, you could easily add "Tell me more." And, in fact, that is exactly what these observations encourage the other person to do. (Again, you may be met with "yup" or "nope" or "I guess so." More on such short replies later.)

Reflect

We discussed reflection briefly in a previous chapter on conflict resolution. As a quick refresher, reflecting is essentially saying back all or part of what someone else has just said to you. Often, people hear their own words differently when spoken back to them by someone else. Reflection also keys in on personal word choice that may have slipped out, but which holds deeper meaning.

A few examples (reflections emphasized):

A: How's your day going?

B: All right, I guess.

A: You *guess?*

A: How's your day going?

B: All right, I guess.

A: Just **all right?**

A: So how did that conversation with your mom go?

B: *uggh* The *worst!*

A: Really? The **worst?**

A: Tell me about the play you're in.

B: I don't know. No one listens to the director.

A: **No** one?

Here again with reflection, you see that an implied "Tell me more" could follow.

If you aren't careful, reflection can sound stilted or forced:

B: I just don't know what to do anymore.

A: You don't know what to do anymore?

This doesn't seem as helpful in getting us to new ground. Maybe this is a place for a shorter reflection paired with an observation or question:

B: I just don't know what to do anymore.

A: You said, 'anymore.' That sounds like you **used to** feel like you knew what to do. [observation]

B: I just don't know what to do anymore.

A: What to **do**? Why do you feel you have to **do** something about the situation? [question]

If done in a natural manner, reflection is a powerful means of helping to keep conversation focused on the speaker, and flowing freely. And as illustrated above, all three of these—questioning, observing out loud, and reflecting—work naturally together.

Embrace Silence

So what about those times when, despite your best efforts, one-word answers still prevail?

Someone once said that silence is golden. We tend to be afraid of silence, but it really isn't so bad. Often, silence is even necessary for people to have time to consider what's been talked about, or to formulate an answer. I couldn't count the times over a dinner that I asked a question or made an observation that initially went unanswered. But, after a little while of just eating, listening to the background music, or observing what was going on around us in the restaurant—and with a few smiles from me in between—a reply *did* come. And a well-thought-out one, at that. It just took some time.

I'm a big fan of *permitting*, as well. That is, verbally allowing something that might otherwise become awkward:

"You know, we don't always have to be talking. I'm happy just to be here with you."

"You don't seem to be in the talkative mood right now, and that's perfectly OK. Do you want to just turn on some music for a while?"

If you hold the place in someone's life, nonverbal communication can bridge silences, as well. I mentioned smiling. You'd be surprised how far a smile really goes toward connecting without words. A shoulder squeeze. A friendly side-bump. A little "finger-puppet" wave. They all say, "I'm here. I know you're here. And I'm glad."

Adding new communication skills to your repertoire can be daunting at first. It takes practice. And that means trial and error. But I can think of few things more worthwhile or rewarding than developing the ability to connect with others on a deeper level.

Questions for Reflection and Discussion:

APPENDIX page 347

CHAPTER 14

Creative Love

A YEAR HAD PASSED since I got caught in that 4th-of-July traffic jam I told you about in the chapter on choosing positivity. Last night, I joined the best people for food and fireworks by the ocean. Unlike many towns, this one has taken to allowing private citizens to light their own fireworks along the shoreline. Not sparklers and bottle rockets, mind you. Real, honest-to-goodness fireworks. And lots *of* them.

Of course, this is all off the books. Fire and police officials "happen" to be very busy in remote parts of town at those hours, it seems— ::wink wink:: —but let's just keep that between ourselves, shall we?

As our little clan made our way along the sidewalks, the town was out in force. Patriotic music played strong and clear as we passed one yard, then seemed to garble like the tuning of a short-wave radio as we walked, only to gradually form itself into another solid tune as we approached the next yard—all accompanied by much boisterous and bad singing. Dogs strained at leashes, barking wildly at the cacophony. Children clustered together on quilts and blankets, bedecked with glowing bracelets and necklaces and halos, all wide-eyed and slack-jawed as they beheld the wonders in the sky.

The sea wall was packed, layers deep. No one seemed to mind. But I navigated my way through the crowd and down the concrete steps, then jumped from the wall to enjoy the spectacle from the rocky beach below. The nearest firework bundles and boxes were a mere twenty feet away from where I sat. *Should be exciting.*

The colors and assortment were dazzling, all fired quite low and seemingly right overhead. But what struck me most was the magnitude of sound. *Whizzing. Screeching. Whirring. **BOOM**ing.* It was the loudest I could recall.

Ever.

At one point, it became overpowering. The sound—not the light—was actually hurting my *eyes*. So I closed them for a moment, placing my hands over them and pressing firmly with my fingertips. That's when the flashback hit.

Ricky.

It was the summer I had graduated from high school. I'd gotten a job at a school for the blind, and I had three "boys" assigned to my care, all of them in for a short-term summer program. In truth, they were each older than I was.

Ricky was 18. Aside from being blind, Ricky had what was then known as pronounced Asperger's Syndrome. This was also accompanied by a form of echolalia. That is, Ricky's tendency was to copy or rephrase what other people said, rather than forming responses with any real personal meaning. So, if one asked Ricky, "Are you having a good day?" he might reply "I'm having a good day"— whether he was having a particularly good day or not.

Ricky was the best. Though he was a year older than I was, he had the affect and voice of a sweet-tempered six-year-old. I was fascinated, but even more determined to have actual communication with him. I was 17 and had no real training. What did *I* know. But I thought it odd that staff just fell into Ricky's patterns, asking predictable and repetitive questions to which they got his predictable and repetitive responses. One day early on, I tried something.

"Hi, Ricky," I said.

Ricky smiled, weaving his head back and forth, which I already understood meant that he was excited and happy. "Hi. Hi, Ricky. Hi," he replied.

"Did you have a good day today?" I asked.

"I had a good day today," Ricky said.

"And what did you like about today?" I continued.

Ricky fell silent. He stopped swaying as if he were listening for something far off. Then he continued his dance, without answering me.

I tried again. "What did you like about today, Ricky?"

He paused again for a moment, then resumed his rhythmical bobbing. "It's nice," he said.

I welled up (much as I'm doing even now as I recall it). Ricky had given a *real* answer!

I continued asking only questions which Ricky could not repeat or rephrase with ease. In what seemed a very short time, Ricky and I were having meaningful exchanges regularly.

I remember the day—or rather the night—that Ricky spoke *first* to me, without my having asked him anything. I had just tucked him into bed and he began to cry. "I'm sad," he said. This was very unusual for someone like

Ricky, to report on how he felt, however obvious.

"Why are you sad, Ricky?" I asked.

"Mom," he said.

"You miss your mom?" I asked, again finding this peculiar behavior, even without any real training.

"I miss my mom," he replied, giving in to his comfort zone of repeating. But that was all right. He'd already told me as much.

Ricky sobbed for a long time that night without any more talk. I stayed with him, lightly raking his hair with my fingertips or squeezing down his arm, which he enjoyed. After more than an hour, he finally fell asleep.

This same scenario played out for the next three nights. Ricky would cry when I put him to bed, and I would stay with him and get him to sleep. After a few days of contemplation at his bedside, I had concocted a plan. There was no way to be sure whether or not it would work, except to just try it and see what happened.

The next day was my day off. I picked up a painter's cap for $5.00. I chose it because it was soft and durable, and the lid was flimsy instead of hard. The following day, I tucked the hat inside my work bag. When bedtime came, sure enough, Ricky began to be homesick. I hated to think about the night before, because I knew the other staff member would not have stayed with him or comforted him. As Ricky began to cry, I took out the hat. I placed it into his hands and helped him feel it. "What do you think this is, Ricky?"

"A shirt," he guessed.

"Nope. It's not a shirt. Good guess. Try again," I urged.

"Try again," he agreed. A few moments later, he said,

"Underwear," then scrunched his face up and giggled like he'd told a naughty joke.

Weeks ago, when Ricky had first arrived, I'd helped him unpack. He had exactly two pairs of yellowed underwear in which the elastic waistbands were stretched and torn. There were two undershirts and one pair of socks, all in similar repair, along with a couple of T-shirts, a pair of jeans and one pair of shorts. This was to last the whole summer. The following day, I had immediately gone shopping and later presented Ricky with a small but new wardrobe—one item at a time. And so it seemed he *did* remember the day I had given him the underwear, as he guessed at what lay in his hands now. The memory of Ricky's reddened face, giggling even as the tears of homesickness streamed down, is still very clear in my mind.

I laughed, too, and replied as if he'd really gotten me with his joke. "*No*, Ricky, it's *not underwear,* silly. It's a hat."

"It's a hat," he said, as if he'd thought of it himself. He felt around the opening and the rim again, trying to make sense of the new revelation.

"It's not just *any* hat, though," I said mysteriously. "It's a *magic* hat."

He didn't reply this time, just listened. I had his attention.

"Here's how it works. You say out loud all of the things you miss and love about home, and the hat remembers them. Then, you put on the hat, and it helps you think good things about what you miss, so you won't be sad while you fall asleep. So, here we go. Let's hold the hat together in our hands and think of as many things as we can think of that you love about home. What's first?"

"Mom," Ricky said, sniffling.

"Good one! And what else do you love about home?" I prompted.

He scrunched his eyes, which were always closed, as if considering. "Cookies."

"Cookies? Nice! And what else?"

"Books." (I hadn't realized before then that, of course, he might like a bedtime story. But I didn't interrupt.) Ricky had already stopped crying as he thought. Before long, his answers became mumbles that meant he was drifting off. I took the hat from his hands.

"OK, now let's put the hat on you, so you can think about all those things you love about home," I said as I pulled the hat over his mop of brown hair. He reached up and touched it, then pulled the covers up and fell asleep. "Good night, Ricky," I said.

The plan had worked. And it continued to work every night thereafter at bedtime.

The 4th of July fell on a Saturday that year, and most parents had come on Friday to get their children for the weekend. Ricky's parents lived in New York, and so had not come. I offered to take Ricky to fireworks that night, even though I was not on shift. This was met with much debate. Bringing a blind student with multiple needs to an event like fireworks? Too upsetting. *And you're not even working.* But no one could argue that Ricky trusted me and was calmer when I was on. And I had clearance to drive the vans. My taking Ricky for the night would also mean that other staff would not have to stay on duty for one student.

And so, we went.

Now, I honestly can't remember how the next turn of events came about. But my sister Shannan wound up coming along. She was sixteen at the time, and had absolutely no experience with special needs. Still, she came. I wondered how she would be with Ricky.

Ricky grew very anxious as the crowds thickened approaching the main event. Shannan and I told him that fireworks would sound very loud and scary, but that it was the *fun* kind of scary. "It's fun," he said, but he didn't seem too sure. Patriotic music played somewhere close by. My sister, without hesitation, asked Ricky if he would like to dance. Ricky's whole life was a dance, in a way— rocking and bobbing and doing the two-step. And so he accepted her offer. She helped him up and fell right into his little two-step, as if it were the cool kids' dance. "You're a *really* good dancer, Ricky," she said." He laughed his giddy laugh. "I'm a *good dancer!*" he shouted, elated to be dancing with a real live girl.

Soon, the first "test" rockets fired, and Ricky was clearly nervous. We sat down on the grass, my sister on one side, and I on the other, pressing in tight on either side so that Ricky would feel safe. "This is going to be a lot of fun!" I assured him. "All of the sounds will be different, because the fireworks look different."

For Ricky, there would be no bursts of color. No designs in the air. No light—only sound. Ricky tilted his face upward in expectancy, as he waited for whatever would happen next, somehow understanding that the noise had come from above him.

Then my sister said something which I'd forgotten until the memory resurfaced last night: "I'll draw pictures on your back of what it looks like."

It was brilliant, really. And moving.

The first legitimate explosions rained overhead. Ricky gasped, but he didn't seem anxious now. I squeezed his hand and said, "Wow! This is scary! Sometimes, it's fun to be scared!" Ricky smiled, with red light shining on his upturned face. Shannan got up and knelt behind Ricky, then wiggled her fingertips over his back in an outward motion approximating what was happening in the sky. The next one screeched out five separate rockets that spiraled away at the end. Ricky squeezed my hand tighter. My sister drew arcs with curlicues up Ricky's back, one at a time. And so it continued.

I really believe that Ricky was having all the fun of going to a scary movie with good friends. He began to laugh out loud, or crouch smaller at the bigger booms, giggling. All the while, I squeezed his hand as my sister drew forms.

THE BEST ADVICE SO FAR:
Tenacious love expressed with creativity can work wonders.

Another shattering *BOOM* brought me back to the present, where I sat there with my fingertips still pressed over my eyes. A few tears escaped as I remembered Ricky and the events of that night.

I wondered where he was, and what he might be doing today.

I wondered if he still had the magic hat.

I wondered if he remembered me, or that night when he'd danced with a girl who smelled nice.

I wondered if he might be at fireworks somewhere even tonight, smiling, squeezing his hand tighter and feeling imaginary fingertips drawing pictures across his back.

What I did *not* need to wonder about—what I was *certain* of—was that time, creative energy and love had been well spent all those years ago.

Questions for Reflection and Discussion:

APPENDIX page 349

CHAPTER 15

Patience

I'M ABOUT TO DATE MYSELF.

When I was growing up, we did not have the Internet. In fact, we did not have home computers at all until I was a teen. When you wanted to know how to tie your tie, you asked around. Or you went to the library and consulted a book.

For factual miscellany, you could call the librarian and ask your question. Who played so-and-so in such-and-such a movie? Or on which day of the week did May 27, 1944 fall? Sometimes, an astute librarian could tell you off the top of her head. Most often, however, she would take down your number and then call you back once she'd researched your question and found the answer.

Calls, by the way, were made from home, not while driving or on a jog. For emergency calls while en route, you pulled over and used your "spare dime" at a station called a pay phone. Oh, and by the way, you actually had to talk to the other person with your voice; there was no breaking up or cancelling plans through text.

If you wanted to see your favorite movie, you usually had to wait until it aired again on television: "Tonight's regularly-scheduled broadcast will not be seen so that we may bring you this special presentation of… 'The Wizard of Oz'!"

Once upon a time, we had to know how to read a map. There were whole books of maps, with legends and grids and markers. They were called atlases. And before a trip, you would mark out your destination in one of these books, and then work out which route would get you there fastest. There was no way to predict construction or traffic. If you hit it, you hit it.

When the Internet finally did make its debut, and the 56k modem became available in the mid-90s, we thought we were in heaven. We simply couldn't believe that we only had to wait a matter of hours instead of days, in order to exchange letters with a friend across the country or the world, or to exchange pictures.

I'm not kidding. It's all true, I swear.

Lest I digress into telling you that we had to walk to school in three feet of snow, uphill both ways, I'll stop. But my reverie wasn't just a spell of nostalgia. I have a point. That is, waiting was the norm. It was expected. It was part of life.

Not so anymore.

There remain a certain few things which still cannot be rushed. Babies. Birthdays. And Christmas. Movie, book and game debuts. A good soufflé. But due to rapid advancements in science and technology, waiting is largely becoming a thing of the past. For the most part, I can have it now. It's stunning, really.

But I sometimes wonder if it's such a good thing after all.

THE BEST ADVICE SO FAR:
Patience is still a virtue.

You see, back when I expected to wait, I was better at it.

And on the occasion when we did *not* have to wait, it was noteworthy. Impressive, not expected.

When the librarian called us back with an answer in only twenty minutes, we thought she was really something and thanked her profusely. We talked about such an event with others: "You wouldn't believe how quickly she got back to me this time! How does she do it?"

We were amazed—more than satisfied—with the "speedy" transfer rate of that 56k modem. The connection time and noises seemed a paltry price to pay for the miracle that would be at our disposal.

Now? We are irritated when the search engine "lags" and takes 20 seconds to return our results.

We've gained the world at our fingertips.

And we've lost the virtue of patience.

I really sound old and stodgy now, don't I? But indulge an old man a bit longer.

Patience, by definition, is the ability to graciously wait. It stands to reason, then, that if I no longer have to wait, I will no longer have opportunities to build patience. And that leaves me being impatient.

Impatient with stoplights that aren't turning when
I will them to.

Impatient with stepping through the options on the automated help system.

Impatient with learning a new skill or sticking with a new undertaking.

Impatient when others do not get out what they are saying fast enough for my liking.

Impatient with the natural foibles and learning curves of my children.

As patience wanes, other things expand to fill the void. Stress. Irritation. Headaches. High blood pressure. Anger.

As I remember it, we were more content with less, back when patience was in vogue. Ah, but alas, technology is here to stay. There is nothing that can be done about it. Or is there? I wonder if there are still things we could do in order to build some patience back into our lives.

Shut off the cell phone at times while driving and practice a little constructive stillness instead.

Scale back daily email checks by half.

Postpone seeing the latest blockbuster film until two weeks after opening night.

Make it a rule not to use express shipping for personal orders online.

Give a verbal six-month commitment before taking on any new venture.

Go to a popular restaurant during peak dinner time without calling ahead, with the express goal of *expecting* to wait.

Find some recipes and make dinners, instead of ordering out or microwaving.

Plant and tend a garden for some of those ingredients.

Reinstate the idea of a "family room," where times are planned solely for talking with my kids or playing a board game together.

Teach a young child to read.

This type of patience building is not passive. It's active. Intentional.

I'm a big proponent of the idea that you can get away with almost anything on a trial basis. So don't go cold turkey on everything at once. Perhaps you could choose one area where you'd like to take the challenge of building purposeful patience, and then do it for a set amount of time. At the end of that time, assess. Did you stick with it? Was it as hard as you thought it would be? Were there any benefits to your sense of well-being? Is there another area in which you might now like to consider making a change?

With some creativity, and a little bit of tenacity,

patience might just make a comeback.

Questions for Reflection and Discussion:
APPENDIX page 351

CHAPTER 16

Avoiding Trouble

I HAD PAID THE $50 BAIL and signed the forms twenty minutes ago. I sat in a chunky, wooden chair with a pea-green "cushion" that crinkled and reminded me of a swimming pool tarp. An infomercial played on the small, tube-model TV that was bolted to a swiveling stand high up in one corner of the stark room. The volume was too low to make anything out, and the hazy picture made it feel more like 3:00 A.M. than just before midnight. Occasionally, the overly enthusiastic hosts would fold into accordion pleats or blip or roll upward on the screen. Sometimes, I took to watching the thin, red seconds hand on the industrial clock make its steady rounds as I waited.

Finally, John came around the corner, escorted by a middle-aged officer with a quirked mouth and a raised eyebrow, causing me to feel as if I too had done something wrong. John smiled sheepishly at me. I smiled back. (I'll talk more about John in later chapters.)

I thanked the officer and clerk, then headed outside with John. "Thanks for doing this," he said. I gave his shoulder a quick squeeze.

Once in the car and on our way, I asked the obvious question: "So what happened?"

John began by explaining that all of the police in the town had made it their sole purpose in life to stalk him and make his life miserable. But, yes, he admitted, he had been drinking. And, yes, he'd been in a car with other boys who'd been drinking. He became more animated as he told the details about how they'd been pulled over, and how panicked they had been, and how the car had been towed. After his story ended, I let the silence speak for a while. John seemed to be listening. "I wasn't *planning* to get in trouble," he said finally. "It just… *happened.*"

As a mentor, I have had up-close and personal dealings with hundreds of kids over the years. Maybe even a thousand by now. And it would be impossible to calculate the number of times I've heard this same refrain: "I wasn't *planning* to!"

THE BEST ADVICE SO FAR:
Don't just *not plan* to get into trouble; plan *not to* get into trouble.

Going through life "not planning to get into trouble" usually leaves us… in a lot of trouble. Trouble is out there. It's lurking, waiting to entice the unwary. Trouble thrives on those who are "not planning to."

Before you nod in agreement, envisioning your wayward nephew or the kid on your block, this doesn't apply merely to teens who are sowing their wild oats.

It applies to dieters who are serious about weight loss.

It applies to married adults who just happen to have that cute, younger coworker—the one who thinks you are incredibly witty and interesting.

It applies to parents who often go to bed with a knot in their stomach, wondering again why so many conversations with their teen end in an argument.

Really, it applies to each of us. Planning *not* to get in trouble requires being self aware and honest enough to know our weaknesses, and then making the difficult choices to put escape routes in place.

Maybe it will mean asking a parent or responsible friend to call and check in with you frequently that night.

Maybe it will mean telling a confidante what you will eat at that party and asking her to keep you to it.

Maybe it will mean saying no to a certain lunch or phone call with that coworker.

Maybe it will mean initiating a week-long "mutual respect" pact with your son or daughter, admitting that you need as much help with it as they do.

In short, planning *not to* get into trouble is *expecting* that trouble will come—because it *will*—and being ready for it when it does.

Questions for Reflection and Discussion:

APPENDIX page 353

CHAPTER 17

Drama

ONE SUMMER, I got a call from Ben, one of the young guys I mentored. He was agitated and had clearly been crying. I asked what was up, and he told me the events of the previous few days.

It seems another boy in town, Tony, was under the impression that his girlfriend had cheated on him—with Ben. This information, as I recall, had been posted on a popular social network site online, ending with the gauntlet being thrown that Ben meet up with Tony and fight. The place and time was set. Though Ben insisted that he had not cheated with Tony's girlfriend, he felt he had no choice but to show up to the fight. As is now commonplace with teens when such skirmishes occur (all of which I still find very odd in social terms), peers were requisitioned to come for the sole purpose of recording "the event" with their cell phones, so that the videos could later be broadcast online.

After a few minutes of exchanged blows, Tony had somehow managed to get Ben into a headlock and threatened to knee him in the face unless he tapped out. Knowing this boy's reputation for fighting dirty—and valuing his own rather nice teeth—Ben did tap out.

He'd "lost" the fight. And it was all on film.

Later at home, bleeding and bruised, Ben took a shower where he cried for some time in anger and frustration. He was overwhelmed. He'd been accused of a crime he hadn't committed. He'd lost a fight with his accuser in front of everyone. That defeat would soon be made public. Kids were already starting to talk.

Everyone would know, he assured me. The entire town would be calling him both a cheater and a loser. He'd already started receiving taunting text messages on his phone. In fact, when our guys' group got together at my house later in the week, a visiting boy chimed in almost immediately with, "Hey, Ben, I heard Tony beat the #*$! out of you."

Here he was, just weeks before beginning high school, and he was already the laughing stock. He felt humiliated. In short, Ben was sure that life as he knew it was over.

This made for quite a discussion among the guys at my house. I'm known for putting people on the spot and asking hard questions. My regular guys have actually come to like this, even request that I ask those hard questions. And I didn't take it easy on the visiting boy, just because he was new to things. My first question was, "Can I ask you, what were you hoping to achieve by bringing that up here, with this being your first visit to the group?" Let's just say things got interesting. In the end, it led to some great discussion and, I trust, some valuable perspective.

When everyone had left, I had a long phone conversation with Ben. I asked him certain questions, to help figure out why he'd gotten into the fight to begin with.

"So, you didn't cheat with Tony's girlfriend and you

told him this."

"Right."

"And, allegedly, he 'beat you' in this fight."

"Yes."

"Does his beating you then prove somehow that you did, in fact, cheat with the girlfriend?"

Ben paused. "Uh… no, I guess not."

"And if you *had* done what he said, but you were determined to have won the fight, would that have proven that you didn't actually cheat with the girl?"

"No."

"So then, am I right in understanding that… the fight had absolutely nothing to do with proving whether or not you cheated with the girl?"

"Gee," Ben said, "I guess not."

As complicated and miserable as things seemed to have gotten for my young friend, my assurance and advice was simple.

THE BEST ADVICE SO FAR:
A fire with no fuel quickly goes out.

With real fires, this seems obvious. An isolated fire, deprived of additional fodder, nearby brush, wind and the like—has no course but to die. It cannot sustain itself. It must have help.

Unfortunately, with the interpersonal fires that start in our lives, we do all the wrong things. We keep them going by talking about the drama to everyone we meet, soliciting their pity at the injustice of it all. We stomp all over them by attempting to backtrack to every person, finding out who heard what from whom in an attempt to correct the story. Heck, we fan the flames with counter campaigns about the unsavory qualities of our perceived opponents, perpetuating the issue or even escalating it.

We do everything but leave the blasted fires alone.

In Ben's case, I advised him to come up with a short, noncommittal response as his reply to anyone who brought it up, something like this:

Pete: "Ben! Tony told me you guys got in a huge fight! He said you cheated with his girlfriend, but he really pounded you and made you call him 'Daddy' before he'd let you go. Is that true?"

Ben: [smiling and in a neutral tone] "You know what? I've made the decision not to talk about it. So I guess whatever he told you is what he told you. I have no problem with Tony."

Now what Pete *really* wanted was controversy. Debate. Drama. Pete wants to fan this flame. But Ben's reply, if he were willing to be consistent with it, leaves nothing for Pete to use as additional fodder. He won't get any more out of Ben. He can't go back and say much to further stir up Tony. He has nothing additional to tell other peers about the situation. Ben looks pretty mature and reasonable, unbothered by whatever may have occurred, and comes off as a generally likable guy.

This fire is quickly becoming embers.

Ben did give this standard reply—and attested that, as promised, people were already losing interest. But some online were still trying to scratch at it and keep the coals hot.

After a few days and with Ben feeling a bit better about

things, I made another recommendation. I suggested that he actually call Tony. He should not try to find Tony and talk to him in a group, or even ask him to step aside to talk. It was equally important that he not try to address him online or in any form such as text that could be copied and sent around. All of these are potential flints, where the pressure of onlookers or the temptation of garnering support might get in the way of two reasonable people talking. No, in order for this to work, Ben would have to man up and call Tony personally. I coached him on what to say, again leaving as little as possible that could be controversial and fuel this fire. I suggested he start the conversation with something like, "Hey, Tony, it's probably weird that I'm calling but… I really don't have a problem with you. And I wanted to know what we could do to end this phone call with you believing that, and the two of us getting along."

Ben asked, "What if he tells me that the only way he'll be willing to drop it is if I call him 'Daddy'?" I snickered at the unlikely scenario plaguing him. But still, I said, "If that happens, then laugh and tell him you will happily call him Your Majesty for the rest of the call if that's all it took to be friends."

And do you know what? Much to his credit as a 14-year-old, Ben did just that. He called Tony and asked what they needed to do to be friends. And to his pleasant surprise, Tony was completely receptive and as willing to be over the drama as Ben was. Tony said that if anyone talked about it further, he would tell them he was cool with Ben and that they were just messing around that day, being stupid.

And that was that. With no fuel left, the fire went out.

But let's not pretend that pubescent boys—or girls—are the only ones to fan the flames when drama arises. Don't we get drawn into the he-said-she-said conversations around the dorm room or the office? Aren't there too many times when one testy word or roll of the eyes from a family member winds up setting the house ablaze, because we treat every battle as cause for a war? How often do we find ourselves at the center of the fray when rumors fly, getting our dander up and letting days and weeks of our lives be ruled by the need to vindicate ourselves at all costs?

When I was in my twenties, in response to having caught wind of some malicious rumors being spread about me, I myself actually mailed out dozens of manila envelopes packed with the equivalent of legal briefs—copies of emails and detailed notes outlining sequences of events, pointing to the logical and irrefutable conclusion that the bad guys were the bad guys, and that I was the good guy. When no one responded to the dossiers, I stood up in a public forum where the guilty parties were present, reading down a list on which I'd written every versions of every accusation that I'd become aware of, and systematically stating that each was both unfounded and untrue. My defense was ironclad. I was Joe of Arc on a quest for Truth and Justice to arise. I ended by essentially decrying the culprits as cowards and liars before walking out.

Yet, for all my efforts, not one person admitted wrongdoing or had a change in stance. No one felt guilty or was browbeaten into begging my forgiveness. I had done nothing more than further fuel the fires of anger and bitterness that had sparked the rumors in the first place, rather than leaving things as they were and letting my reputation speak for itself over time. I had simply drawn additional people into the drama—some of whom had been unaware of the rumors prior to my missive—and had given an even larger audience more reasons to talk a while longer.

The rumors, of course, died out after I let them, and today hold absolutely no bearing on my current emotions or state of affairs. Truthfully, I can't even remember some of the key players' names. I really do look back and roll my eyes at it all. How could I have thought that stomping and thrashing in a fire would put it out? If only I had realized then the value in the advice I'm giving you here, I could have saved myself a lot of grief. And postage.

In a nutshell, here's the plan I've found works best. Smile. Be gracious. Don't slander or show ill will toward others. Give a standard response to any who inquire, simply stating that you've chosen not to fuel the fire by talking further about the issues. Express your hopes that everyone will work it out in time.

The best I can figure, people love drama because their own daily lives are so mundane, so devoid of clear purpose and passion, that the blaze of controversy provides a feeling something like being alive for a while. That being the case, when one fire begins to die down, such people quickly grow bored and restless again, and scuttle off in search of someone else's more heated conflict to dazzle them for a while.

Doing nothing when drama arises seems to go against everything crying out inside of us. But as I told Ben—and as I myself have practiced happily since the above-noted debacle—doing nothing is actually the most likely and expedient route to putting out fires and restoring your own sense of peace.

One last thought here. To truly live this advice will require a willingness to sidestep the drama that comes your way—even when you are *not* the topic. Somewhere in all of us is the strange desire to be in the know and to dish the dirt. But you can expect your own fires to fizzle sooner when you become known as someone who isn't interested in helping to burn down your neighbors' houses.

Questions for Reflection and Discussion:

APPENDIX page 355

CHAPTER 18

Motives

IREMEMBER ONE PARTICULAR DAY when I was maybe seven years old. Even at this age, my siblings and I had specific chores involving some pretty hardcore tasks at times. Dust whole rooms (with polish). Lug firewood from our horse barn out back and stack it in a room by the woodstove, devoted solely to such purpose. On the day in question, my father had been upset about something or other that was out of place or not up to standard in the house. I don't remember where he drove off to, but before he left the house, he said, "Get this place together by the time I get back! No short cuts! And I mean it better sparkle!"

I was in charge of the family room. I dusted around the spindled backs of chairs. I vacuumed the carpet and then scanned the floor again, picking up with my fingers any stray lint or tenacious particles the vacuum had left behind. I straightened the books on the bookshelf, thinking in my 7-year-old, perfectionist brain that placing them in order of height along each shelf was important somehow to really doing it up. When I was done, I stood back and looked at my work. Looked pretty spiffy. (I hoped my father would think so.) Yet something was lacking. There was one thing left to do.

It just.

Didn't.

Sparkle.

I went into a craft kit and returned with a small, clear plastic vial. I carefully placed pieces of its contents—one by one—on different surfaces of the room. On flat upright surfaces, such as the front of the fireplace mantel, the sides of the piano, or the wall, I used the tiniest amounts of glue to affix the glitter. It is hard to assess, from an adult perspective looking back, just how long this finishing-touch process took me, but I would think a half hour is a reasonable estimate.

I stepped back again. Sure enough, that room sparkled! Especially if you weaved and bobbed your head around. And if you knew what to look for. I was filled with the exhilaration of the kind of true pride that accompanies a job well done. I could not wait for my parents to see, eager for the praise my extra measures would certainly warrant.

Eventually, my father came back. He walked around the house silently, surveying. I stood tall, on the threshold between the kitchen and the family room, rocking up and down on tiptoes in anticipation of the moment when the sparkles caught his eye.

You cannot imagine my dejection when he scanned the room quickly, then turned back the other direction without comment.

"Wait!" I interjected. "Didn't you notice?"

"Notice what?" came the dry reply.

"The… *SPARKLES!*" In my mind's eye, I'm raising my eyebrows too high, looking a lot like Fozzy Bear from the Muppet Show. In my mind's eye, I've got jazz hands to the side, as if to say, "Check it out! Incredible, right?"

The moments between that tip-off and my father realizing I'd actually decorated the room with glitter are a blur. Suffice it to say, it didn't go over so well.

"Why the anecdote?" you ask.

I recount this story to illustrate my next bit of advice.

THE BEST ADVICE SO FAR:
Motive is more important than behavior or outcome.

So, gluing glitter to household furnishings… not so great. Motive? Stellar!

If you practice this until it becomes a natural part of your thought processes, you will have added a powerful tool to your arsenal when it comes to interpersonal relationships. The fact is, we aren't always going to be thrilled about what other people do, particularly when what they do conflicts with our own goals, ideas or comfort. The natural tendency is to focus on how we have been inconvenienced by someone's actions, and so our responses come out as irritation, anger and criticism.

So imagine. Someone has done or said something you don't like. Your mom made family plans without consulting you, and you've already made plans with a friend. Your boss changed insurance policies to a plan that doesn't include your primary care doctor. Your daughter just asked you how you could be a Republican and still say you care about education or the environment. Your pulse quickens, and you breathe in a slow breath that inflates your lungs like the hood of a cobra ready to strike.

Instead of focusing on *what* your mom or boss or daughter has done, stop and ask yourself, "*Why* did they do or say that?"

You see, the grounded teen responds to *what* his parents did as if reality is that he hates them and they hate him. But stopping to ask, "*Why* did they ground me?" may reveal an answer that makes the *what* bearable. Assuming that mom and dad are not fueled by pure cruelty and are not just egomaniacs drunk on their own inflated sense of power, an answer closer to the truth is likely "They think it's going to motivate me to make better decisions before I become an adult." Whether their methods are perfect, or even successful, is not as important as understanding their motives—their heart in the matter.

Whenever I am asked to facilitate conflict resolution between others, I will first ask each person to describe the situation from his or her perspective. I will always follow this up with something like, "Now tell me *why* you think he did that." This usually catches people by surprise. Often, they haven't even considered the why. And when they do, it's not uncommon for people to feel a little sheepish or to laugh. At the very least, a realization of the answer to this question almost always throws water on the coals of a fire.

Questions for Reflection and Discussion:

APPENDIX page 301

CHAPTER 19

Vital Signs

F EW THINGS ARE AS FRUSTRATING as
having a heated discussion (a.k.a. argument) that
doesn't end well. Adrenaline courses. Blood pressure
spikes, making your eyes feel swollen and tight in their
sockets. Words fly. Emotions flare. Now nobody is talking.

No barrel of monkeys.

As if this weren't grueling enough, many people then
decide to repeatedly replay the events mentally, getting
angry all over again at how unfair it all was, or fabricating
a version in which they had said something much more
clever and movie worthy.

Because people are individuals and do not always share
the same perspective, conflict is an inevitability. But there
are some simple strategies that can keep disagreements
from becoming full-blown fights.

If we don't deliberately and regularly practice patience,
emotions can quickly get the best of us and escalate an
already tense situation. When emotions turn a negative
direction, your body knows. You may begin to actually feel
your heartbeat (which is not the norm). Or your breathing
changes. You might even realize you are holding your
breath while the other person is speaking.

THE BEST ADVICE SO FAR:
When conversations become difficult, being aware of physical changes and reporting them openly can help calm things down.

Whatever change you feel, simply state what it is:

"I can feel my heart racing."

"I just realized I've been holding my breath."

"My eyes sting."

Something about making those changes known out loud shifts the focus from words to the real people involved. It also creates some space between word volleys by introducing responses that are out of step with the direction of the argument. Look at the following sample argument:

Craig: "…but I've had the same curfew since I was 12!"

Mom: "I'm the mother. You're still the kid. And that means that I still get to make the rules around here."

Craig: "I'm not a kid, I'm 17! Nine o'clock is ridiculous for a 17-year-old."

Mom: "So now I'm ridiculous, am I? Well, it's about to get a lot more ridiculous when I make it eight o'clock!"

Notice how emotions are escalating. Notice also that actual resolution doesn't seem to be coming any time soon. Now, let's interject some of our new advice into this argument:

Craig: [pause] "I just realized I haven't breathed since the last time I spoke."

Do you see how this *must* change the course of this argument? Mom can't really continue her emotional escalation here with, "Not *breathing* now, eh? Well, now your curfew is *seven* o'clock!" Craig's honest report of his physical condition is all but certain to elicit a different kind of response from mom.

A few additional thoughts are in order.

This is not a "tactic" to be used as emotional manipulation. Making up dire-sounding physical symptoms ("I feel like I'm going to pass out") in order to shut someone down or get your way is actually counter-productive, and frankly, immature. What's more, if this is a habit (or becomes one), the boy-who-cried-wolf syndrome will prevent this piece of advice from having any effectiveness whatsoever. The goal of this advice is to foster more honest communication, which in turn interrupts emotionally-charged "word slinging." If the goal becomes emotional manipulation, the likely response will be, "Oh boy! Here we go again with the drama!"

It's important to focus on what you yourself are feeling. If you are an active participant in the conflict at hand, it's probably best to avoid pointing out physical changes you notice in the other person. (You can imagine how, "Your face is getting all red, you know" might not help an already difficult situation.) And, in conjunction with other advice found in this book, state what you are noticing about yourself in terms of what you feel, not what the other person is "making you feel." For instance, "My head is pounding" not "You're giving me a headache."

Finally, I'm not siding with Craig or against mom here! If mom were to take this advice and say something like, "I hear myself raising my voice now and my eyes hurt," Craig's next response must change.

Questions for Reflection and Discussion:

APPENDIX page 357

144

CHAPTER 20

Softening Blows

"IF YOU DON'T HAVE ANYTHING NICE TO SAY, don't say anything at all." You'll notice that this timeless piece of advice is not in bold type. It is not part of what I consider The Best Advice So Far. That is not because I consider it bad advice in principle, or that I'm not wholeheartedly behind the sentiment. I do not dole out this advice for one reason: it is unrealistic. Even in a utopian society, where every person decided to speak only "nice" things, the advice wouldn't be practical. That is because not-so-nice events are an inherent part of the world in which we live, and honest communication requires that we talk about them.

However, though a particular topic may not be bursting with roses and sunshine, we can approach the delivery in a way that nods to the time-worn advice above. We can *be* nice, even if the message isn't quite. In twenty years of mentoring, perhaps the most quoted advice I've given pertains to one such strategy.

THE BEST ADVICE SO FAR:
When you have a potentially
controversial topic at hand,
throw a bone first.

Don't throw the book out just yet. I'm not crazy. Let me explain.

Picture it. Pit bull. Angry pit bull. Drooling. Barking. Baring sharp teeth. He is in the mood to rumble. You want to get by with as little pain as possible. Having immense wisdom and foresight, you have brought the doggy bag (I know—my puns are incredible) of bones from the delicious, tender ribs you had for lunch. Said pit bull makes a go at you, snarling. Just then, you produce a bone, brandish it and throw it. As menacing and mean as he might be feeling, that dog has just been thwarted. He can't resist the smell. He quickly decides the bone will be more satisfying than your rear end. He slobbers off toward the bone, leaving you to pass unscathed.

As it relates to interpersonal matters, throwing a bone is offering a positive, related and sincere complement to soften the blow before getting into the messy bit.

Look at the three key elements with me: *positive, related, sincere.*

Let's say your [spouse/boyfriend/girlfriend] is starting to drive you crazy by calling you 25 times during the day to ask what you are doing, where you are, when you will be back. Their ring tone goes off. Again. You find yourself sighing. You let the call go to voice mail—along with the nine before it. Something has to be done.

Devoid of any helpful advice, you see your love later on that evening:

Love: "What's going on? I called 15 times and texted 10! I *know* you got them! I can't believe you'd *ignore* me! *Are you cheating on me*?"

[Recall image of pit bull here.]

You: "I'm not cheating on you, but it's tempting when you annoy the bejeezus out of me by ringing my phone six thousand times a day."

OK. Stop. Wait. That wasn't even a little nice. Let's rewind and try again without going so overboard, yet still without throwing a bone.

You: "I'm sorry, I just can't answer that many calls a day. Do you think you could keep it to one or two?"

All right. Nicer. But you do realize that you are still about to get your face ripped off, and how.

Instant replay, where you are armed with your bone-throwing advice:

Love: "What's going on? I called 15 times and texted 10! I *know* you got them! I can't believe you'd *ignore* me! *Are you cheating on me*?"

You: [little kiss] "You know what? I really love the fact that you want to talk to me so much throughout the day. It makes me realize how much you care about me. I just get into a flow with things and can't always pick up. But I'm here now, so let's catch up."

By throwing this positive bone, you may just have saved your pretty face.

But don't overlook the other elements. The bone must be related to the topic at hand. Consider the following interaction:

Dad: "Where have you been? It's 15 minutes past your curfew, young lady!"
Young Lady: "Gee, dad, what's that scent you're wearing? I dig it!"

While positive, this response is undoubtedly not helping matters.

Instant replay:

Dad: "Where have you been? It's 15 minutes past your curfew, young lady!"

Young Lady: "Thanks for being worried about me and staying up to make sure I got in safe, Dad. Honestly, I don't know how, but I just lost track of time. Sorry."

Finally, the bone must be sincere. Smarminess works against honest communication, and may even rile the pit bull more. In putting thought to a sincerely positive aspect of the person or situation, you are also assuring that you yourself are entering the discussion with a reminder about the good in the other person, making it less likely that you will resort to comments that will be hurtful.

Questions for Reflection and Discussion:

APPENDIX page 359

CHAPTER 21

Asking Questions

S OCRATES WAS KNOWN for asking questions. Socrates is generally considered to have been a pretty smart guy. So I'll ramp up the importance of this piece of advice by saying that I got it from Socrates.

THE BEST ADVICE SO FAR:
Asking the right kind of questions works better than making statements.

If you were to have asked Socrates, he would have told you that not all questions are created equal. Some questions are wasted questions. I've known a few kids through the years that were notorious question wasters. One in particular comes to mind who, upon seeing his mother's skin glowing red around distinct bathing suit lines, asked, "Did you get sunburned?" People typically waste questions when they would like to start a conversation but find themselves at a loss for what to say. This sometimes happens when there is tension between people, but no one will say so. A wasted question may be a sign that someone *wants* to resolve the conflict but doesn't know how to begin.

Some questions are rhetorical. In a conflict situation,

such a question has the effect of a negative statement, and does not register as a question at all. Behind the ever-popular "Do I look stupid to you?" is the statement "You seem to think I'm stupid, and I get very angry when people think I'm stupid." The equally ubiquitous "What in the world were you thinking?" is really a thinly-veiled "You blew it big time!" And "Were you raised in a barn?" is little more than "Close the door, you inconsiderate dolt." As such, rhetorical questions don't really count as questions for the purposes at hand. It should also be noted that adding a clever, question-like appendage to a statement does not magically make it count as a question.

Consider:

"You take great pleasure in humiliating me, don't you?"

"Well, this is fine mess you've made of things, isn't it?"

You will earn no points with these. Come now. You know better. (Don't you?)

Let's explore a few varieties of questions that *do* tend to aid in discussion.

Questions of a truly inquisitive nature are generally helpful. These questions show real interest in the other person. They are an admission that you do not claim to understand all the facts and are a reassurance that you have not yet drawn any conclusions. Look for ways to replace statements and opinions with inquisitive questions, and you will remove bricks from walls of defensiveness. So, instead of exclaiming to your son, "I can't believe you got an F in English!" try "Where do you think things went wrong in English this term?" And rather than telling your parents, "You just hate all my friends," you might ask "Can you tell me what in particular you don't like about Joey?" More specific questions will keep things focused. But don't abuse specific inquisitive questions by using them merely as an excuse to be nosy.

Another useful type of question is the leading question. A leading question is used to elicit the truth of a statement from another person, rather than stating the facts yourself. Mastering the use of leading questions can drastically change the dynamic of conversations. It is a skill, and thus, it takes practice. But the practice offers a major payoff.

You see, when emotions are roiling, much of what we hear is deflected from invisible walls of defensiveness. We are too busy thinking about how hurt we are, or planning what we will say next (or imagining how good it would feel to kick that kneecap) to really hear what the other person is saying. They are the enemy in those moments and, as such, their words are weapons. We try to protect ourselves from those weapons by downplaying, tuning out or dismissing their words as biased, ridiculous or petty.

A leading question, however, is a Trojan horse. By its nature, it has the power to get to the other side of a defensive wall. It also sinks in deeper than a statement could, because the truth of the answer must first travel through the heart and mind and then out of the mouth of the other person.

What does a leading question look like? Here are a few examples of statements reworked into leading questions:

Statement: "I'm really disappointed in you."

Leading question: "Can you imagine how I might be feeling about this right now?"

Statement: "You have a big problem with lying."

Leading question: "Would you say most people consider you a truthful person?"

Statement: "You were really mean to me last night."

Leading question: "How do you think our conversation went last night?"

Hitting someone with lots of facts or opinions can quickly devolve into talking *at* someone, rather than talking *with* them. Such a barrage of statements can be tuned out easily and indefinitely, with the speaker being none the wiser. However, it is nearly impossible to ignore a leading question because, by its nature, it requires a response. And responses are a good sign that real communication is happening. Perhaps the most effective part of learning to use leading questions is that the truth of the response is revealed by the other person and not by you. You are not "the bad guy." Your words are not the gavel.

And so you actually stand a good chance of getting the truth across *while* maintaining the ability to be sympathetic and encouraging as harsh realities are brought to light.

One additional note. Just as rhetorical questions are really just statements disguised as questions, leading questions can come in the form of an invitation. For instance, there is not much difference in effect between "How do you think our conversation went last night?" and "Tell me about how you think our conversation went last night." Both versions imply the need for a response.

We'll revisit the topic of asking good questions in upcoming chapters.

Questions for Reflection and Discussion:

APPENDIX page 361

CHAPTER 22

Respect

URING MY TEEN YEARS, I attended a school where, for reasons I still haven't quite figured out, competition was a higher priority than learning. I don't mean the healthy sort of competition where better students rub elbows with marginal students to somehow "bring up the pack." I mean grass-in-the-teeth, slice-your-throat kind of competition. I was a straight-A student. All right… I was a *straight-A-PLUS* student. And that meant that the plain old straight-A students hated me.

From the normal arenas like sports, to the bizarre— like who could not only memorize a poem, but rattle it off the fastest without error—competition was the fuel that ran the machine. We even had regular classroom competitions to see who could find a certain page or reference in a book the fastest. And, as if this in-house pressure cooker weren't enough, they also made it a practice to compete against other similarly minded schools on a regular basis.

To this day, anything that smacks of organized competition still gives me the willies. Don't even get me started on child pageants. ::shudder::

As I said, I was a capable student. And I was fairly good at a variety of arts, as well. So I was a prime target when these inter-school competitions came around.

My freshman year, I was entered in ten events: two piano solos, pencil art, debate, choir, vocal solo, vocal duet, monologue, persuasive speech and spelling bee. Why did I enter so many categories? I suppose the answer is twofold: perfectionism and guilt. I'd like to say that I entered because of my love for the arts. I did not. You see, it was expressly and routinely stated in my school that "to whom much is given, much shall be required." That apparently meant that being *able* to do a thing obligated one to do it. (If this sounds even somewhat reasonable to you, I implore you to read the chapter on "Saying No" and to begin the un-brainwashing process immediately.)

Did I mention that each of these individual events took a great deal of preparation? Did I mention I was entered in ten?

One day in class, as competition deadlines were nearing, my English teacher announced that we still needed an entrant for poetry recitation. He smiled as if he were going to tell a dirty joke and looked at me. "Mr. Tyler…" he said, eyebrow arched.

I looked at him coolly, drawing a slow breath. "I'm already entered in ten categories. I can't do any more." This was by no means an end to the matter. It was only a gauntlet.

"Sure you can," he continued through his smug smile, his voice equally steeled. "To whom much is given…"

My throat felt constricted. This was a battle of wills. And there was an audience. "I'm not doing it," I said, eyes narrowing.

His grin twisted and his nostrils flared like a bull ready to charge. All at once, a stick of chalk was flying, barely missing my head to break against the back wall. "Well, if you're going to have a bad attitude about it, we might as well just cancel the whole competition!" he bellowed and then stalked out of the room.

It's hard to describe exactly how I felt in that moment. Exhilarated (because I'd stood my ground and won). Furious. Unappreciated. One thing is certain. In that moment, I hated him.

That was on a Friday. I spent the night at a friend's house. The phone rang. My friend went to answer it. He returned and handed it to me, mouthing with warning eyes the name of our English teacher. The wave of loathing flooded me again. How dare he call me about this? And on a weekend! And while I'm at someone else's house! *This had better be an apology*, I threatened mentally.

"Hello," I said blankly.

"Mr. Tyler." I remained silent. He continued, "You put me in a very difficult situation today. You didn't respect me." His voice was pure condescension.

They say that "hell hath no fury like a woman scorned." Well, scorned women everywhere needed to take a back seat, because a whole new level of fury was being invented as he spoke.

"You *are* going to do the poetry recitation, Mr. Tyler. I already submitted your name. You're doing Poe's 'The Raven.' You'll do a great job with it."

My friend, apparently alarmed that I had ripped through my skin and was now a disembodied homicidal inferno, took the phone. "Hold on," he spoke into the receiver.

Next thing I knew, my friend's father was standing near me, talking on the phone. I had gotten back into my body somehow, though the process managed to drain all the blood from it. My feet were cold. His father spoke in a gentle yet firm tone to my teacher. It was short. Very short. And then he hung up the phone without further discussion. His simple words made an indelible mark on me.

THE BEST ADVICE SO FAR:
You can't demand respect.
You have to earn it.

Carefully considering, and then redefining, terms is extremely beneficial here. Without question, you *can* demand some things. If you hold the proper reins of authority over someone, you can demand compliance. You can demand obedience. You can demand that certain words be spoken. You can even demand that those words be delivered with a demeanor and tone that approximates sincerity. You can punish or manipulate someone into conforming to a certain response that you prefer. But none of these things constitutes—nor fosters—respect. In fact, demanding compliance almost always results in a lack of respect.

This removes all forms of "You need to respect me!" from the table. It is an invalid statement. Instead, try "I wish you would respect me" or "I feel like you don't respect me." Those are honest communication. Better still, respect the other person by giving solid reasons rather than "because I said so" or "because I'm the boss." Let go of being able to demand respect. Instead, ask yourself, *What do I need to do in order to earn this person's respect?* If you're really up for a new beginning, ask *them*: "What do you think it would take for me to earn your respect?"

Many times, parents or school authorities will ask me to speak to a child or teen about an issue on which the adult has "demanded respect" and gotten nowhere. The adult is often amazed at the positive results of my conversation with the kid. "How did you do it? What did you say?"

There is no magic in what I may have said. But there is a kind of magic in the approach I use in relationships and, consequently, in how that causes the teen and I to discuss a given topic. And that approach isn't, "Hey, could you just do what they want this once so I can look good?" I believe that respect doesn't only aim upward. It is a partnership. Each person respects the other, by listening, explaining, keeping the *relationship*—and not the "issue"—in focus. In all my years of teaching, I never had to send someone out of the room or threaten them in order to elicit good behavior. Nor was I a pushover. Students learned. They even liked to learn. Because I respected them, they respected me.

For many people, this shift in thinking and approach will seem like letting go of an ace up the sleeve. It will feel like a loss of power, handing it over to another person. But remember that the "power" of demanding respect is only ever an illusion. In reality, working toward earning mutual respect gives power to the *relationship*. And that is real power that will work for everyone.

[Note: After many years and a lot of growth on both our parts, that English teacher and I are now good friends who laugh and shake our heads about those days!]

Questions for Reflection and Discussion:

APPENDIX page 363

CHAPTER 23

Compliance

I LIVED IN A GATED COMMUNITY where residents were promised "immaculately manicured grounds." That's what the lease said anyway. Call me crazy, but "immaculate" seems a lofty claim to uphold. Still, there it was in black and white.

In reality, patches of matted brown grass made a piecemeal quilt of the lawns. Discourteous residents frequently left behind little "surprises" left by their dogs. And dandelions teemed. The effect of the latter on me, for some reason, was similar to seeing pictures of the Surinam toad—you know, the one that hatches its young from widening pores across its back. Disturbing.

Just before the infestation became utterly unbearable, the landscaping company would show up in their green and white trucks, spreading out across the property. This did little to solve the doggie doo issue, except perhaps to scatter it over a wider area where it might act as fertilizer. However, areas of dead grass were soon disguised with some sort of unnaturally green chemical spray. And the dandelions were beheaded by the whizzing metal blades of mowers, or flattened under the weight of their tractor-like wheels.

The following day, with the smell of freshly cut grass still lingering, you'd look around and think you were living in Beverly Hills. If you didn't look too closely, it might even *seem* immaculate. But before two days had gone by, the trampled weeds began to rear their heads like waking cobras. And by week's end, the lawn was once more choked by swarms of Hydra so numerous, even Hercules would take one look and throw in the towel.

THE BEST ADVICE SO FAR:
Clipped weeds soon return.

Don't think it isn't tempting to end the chapter there, leaving you to scratch your head at how this fits in with the rest of the advice in this book. If only life's biggest challenge were an ugly lawn.

Forcing compliance is an awful lot like thinking you've beaten a weed by hacking away at the part that offends you. Don't like the angry words your teenage son just shouted at you? Send him to his room. Caught him smoking weed with friends? Take away his phone, Internet and car for a month, and forbid him to have any contact with the offending compadres. Think you're girlfriend might be tempted to cheat with one of her guy friends? Guilt her with the silent treatment or bombard her with rage until she agrees not to hang out with him anymore.

You do *this* so that they will do *that.* The problem goes away. Simple, right?

I mentioned in a previous chapter the idea that *what* someone does is far less important than *why.* This applies here, as well, though from a different angle.

It's easy to fixate on effecting an immediate change in another's behavior by using punishment, emotional manipulation or other tactics. Getting someone to behave the way we'd like makes us feel settled and in control again for a while. If we don't have to look at a problem, we can imagine that it doesn't exist. But realize that such an approach is very me-centered, and not particularly focused on the well-being of the other person. This is especially easy to justify to ourselves when the other person is being a jerk. But jerk or no, make no mistake about the fact that forcing compliance is still about *me* and putting my comfort first.

The image comes to mind of the archetypal father from some vague yesteryear who, upon hearing his son swear, took the lad out behind the woodshed exclaiming, "This is going to hurt me more than it hurts you," and then proceeded to administer a sound switching to the kid's backside. Sounds noble, but I can tell you from experience that the aforementioned claim is nonetheless untrue.

As I'm writing this, I get the feeling that jaws are slowly clenching and heartbeats are quickening in parents and teachers who think I just don't get it. Please know that I am not against establishing clear guidelines for behavior and issuing consequences for poor choices. I'm actually very much in favor of these things and have used them myself. I'm simply saying that they are not *enough*. Alone, they do not solve the problem.

Consider a young man who uses and sells drugs. When sales are lacking, he also takes the five-finger discount on electronics and other gadgetry and hocks them on the street. Now, if the police finally nab this fellow and put him in prison, his confinement will prevent him from using or selling drugs. Likewise, we can assume with relative surety that he will not steal during the term of his incarceration. Thus, we can now say that he is no longer a drug addict or thief. The end.

I should think the problem with this logic is evident.

First, I can tell you, based on the accounts of many I've known personally, that even prison does not necessarily prevent the procurement and distribution of nearly anything behind bars. I can also assert with equal confidence that I've never known jail time of any length to cure a thief or rehabilitate an addict. Once they hit the pavement, cell phones are dialed, familiar circles are reestablished, and old patterns take over right where they left off.

Why then is it so much more difficult to see that banishing my son to his room for an outburst of bad language doesn't get at the underlying anger or frustration inside of him? In fact, might it even be exacerbating it?

Similarly, grounding a teen for drug use (in essence, imposing a prison sentence for a certain length of time) does nothing toward addressing an addiction, or the *cause* of seeking an escape. I can tell you with authority that, while you might even be successful for a time at curbing such behaviors by tightening the reins, the problem will not have gone away. Just like those clipped dandelions, the roots are very much alive, waiting for the right moment to resurface. They will blow silent seeds or travel underground if they must, springing up in some unseen part of the yard. But make no mistake—they will emerge. You can control where someone goes outside of the house, but you cannot control what they do during every moment of private time in bedrooms and bathrooms. Where drug use might have been rooted in control issues (and often it is), that sense of control may instead begin to evidence itself in other body addictions associated with control. Eating disorders. Pornography. Cutting.

Further, to keep someone locked into a relationship, by making it all but impossible for them to be around "other options," is not in any way a reflection nor a guarantee of their actual fidelity and love. As is the nature of so many attempts to force conformity, the very measures used in hopes of gaining the outcome I want become the catalyst for pushing someone in the opposite direction.

I don't know how many of us have someone in our life from whom we will hear the unadorned truth about ourselves. For those who may not, perhaps you will allow me to be a temporary surrogate here and say, if getting your own way through manipulation and tantrums is your *modus operandi*, the behavior that needs changing is not someone else's but your own.

In closing, let me reiterate to parents and other caregivers in a bit more detail that, in many instances, implementing consequences is necessary. At these times, however, I find it best to leave as little to the heat of the moment as possible. Lashing out with impromptu punishments (e.g., "You're grounded from everything for a month!") is rarely constructive or effective in addressing the root problem. I suggest having a family meeting (or a one-on-one sit down) at a time when things are calm and behavior is not an immediate issue. At that time, establish a "consequence book." In it, brainstorm together some key behaviors that all agree tend to be recurring issues. By brainstorming,

I really mean asking, "What do you think are the areas where you wind up getting into trouble?" accompanied by some prompts as to specific, recent examples if necessary. Then, together, come up with reasonable—*and related*—consequences for each behavior and write them down (again, asking first what seems reasonable, and steering as necessary). Be specific. For instance, if the issue is rude and inappropriate arguing, perhaps an appropriate and related consequence (however unhip and outdated it may seem) might be missing a preferred activity in favor of staying in and having a conversation together about it. So that entry might look like this:

OFFENSE: rudeness / inappropriate arguing

CONSEQUENCE: miss weekend activity and have
a talk with mom / dad

Whatever the case, the important thing isn't so much the nature of the consequence itself, as that everyone agrees on what it is and that it is deemed reasonable. Then, the next time the behavior occurs and goes unchecked, there is no need for emotional upheaval. You simply refer to the book and follow through on what was already decided and agreed upon. This makes consequences a *choice*—not a whim. And no one has to be the bad guy.

A few more thoughts on this. If you decide to implement "the book" and you find down the line that you've left some behaviors out, make the catch-all consequence a weekend discussion (preferably at a time that works for everyone, not just the parent) with the express goal of adding that behavior and consequence to the book. In essence, the first one is a "freebie." Including everyone in the process of identifying negative behaviors and deciding upon reasonable consequence does wonders toward decreasing the frequency of those behaviors, while keeping emotional flares to a minimum and reinforcing the idea of personal choice rather than punishment.

Really want to put yourself out there? Allow your son or daughter to suggest consequences for *your* telltale bad behaviors, as well.

Still thinking I'm talking through my hat? Please know that I did this very thing with the two volatile teens for whom I served as guardian over a combined span of nearly four years, and with good success I might add.

Even with such measures in place, this *still* does not automatically get at the underlying factors influencing behavior, without the addition of a crucial next step. Consequences should always be more about creating down time and space—as free from emotional bias as possible, during which to have deeper conversations about those "roots" of behavior—and less about controlling actions or forcing conformity.

Questions for Reflection and Discussion:

APPENDIX page 365

CHAPTER 24

People vs. Problems

L ET ME TELL YOU ABOUT JERRY.
I met Jerry when I was working in an inner-city high school program. The program met in the basement of the school and was funded on a grant as an experiment. The kids in the program were teens on parole or probation, or who were in gangs, or who were students otherwise at high risk for truancy. The aim of the program was to find ways to keep them in school.

My first day on site, I pored over files, choosing out my first students. My goal was to identify and connect with those I felt were at critical risk level from among the already high-risk population. Jerry was a clear frontrunner.

Jerry was 17. They'd told him he was a junior; but as far as actual credits, he was only in high school because of his age and the special nature of the program. Jerry was on a strict, court-ordered probation for a number of crimes. He had already done time. One of the stipulations of his probation — the only thing preventing him from going immediately back to lock-up — was that he attend school daily. He was to obey the rules. He was to attend all classes assigned to him.

The problem was, Jerry could not read.

Jerry's file showed that he had received years of state-funded special services in reading and math. Yet, his last available test scores from only a few years earlier showed that he was still on a first-grade reading level. My priority with Jerry would not be counseling. It would not even be academic support, per se. My goal had to be to try to teach this near-man to read past "Do you like my little dog?"

I knew I could succeed—that *he* could succeed—if I could get him in the chair. My roster was complete. I went to meet the kids. Jerry was my first visit. I entered a classroom, where the teacher lounged with his feet up on his desk, and students looked at the pictures and stats of sports teams in daily papers strewn across tables. Heat began to rise in my chest. I hoped this was some sort of break time and not the norm. "I'm here to see Jerry," I announced.

Heads turned toward a lanky African-American boy, with half-closed eyes that said at once that he trusted no one. Jerry's eyebrows raised self-consciously but his face remained a stone. He did not look toward the doorway where I stood. I felt for him immediately. "Hi, everyone. Hi, Jerry. Why don't you at least come out in the hall for a second so I can tell you *why* I'm here to see you." He pushed himself up roughly, the waist of his pants hanging just above his knees and the rest pooling about his sneakers in seeming bolts of denim. He sauntered to the door with a look of defiance, almost threatening. He still would not look at me, his eyes seeming to trace an invisible, zigzag line on the floor. Once he was outside the classroom, I quietly closed the door. Even leaning against the wall in a slouch, staring straight ahead, he towered over me.

I felt confident. Excited. I was *going* to teach this kid to read. More importantly, I was determined to help him see his own worth as a person. I had my work cut out for me.

"Hey, Jerry. I'm Erik. It's my first day. Listen— I read your file. So I know a little *about* you. But I don't know *you.* I hope I will. But right now, I want to ask you to take a risk with me. Look at it as a sort of dare."

He glanced *toward* me, though not quite at me. At least it was something. I kept going. "I want you to give me two weeks, an hour each day, to work with you on reading."

That was it. He was already shaking his head and gesturing vehemently, an acrid look on his face. "Naw, naw, naw. I'm not *[expletive]* going to your *[expletive]* retard classes, man!"

The window was closing. I had to act fast. I pushed forward. "Jerry, it won't be the same as before. I promise. Give me two weeks. Just ten days. And if you don't feel like you are reading much better by then, you can quit."

"I can *already* quit," he countered. "You can't *make* me do *nothin'*."

He started walking away down the hall. I drew in a breath, gearing for the big guns. I hated to have to use them, but I knew it was for his best. I followed him. "Jerry, your file says you are on probation and that you have to go to classes and follow the rules. If you don't come to my class, I will have to call your probation officer and tell him that you aren't following the program."

He stopped.

You could feel the air change, almost crackle. He spun on his heels to face me and looked me dead in the eyes for the first time. "A'ight. " It sounded like a question.

A menacing challenge more than assent.

"Good decision," I said. "You won't be sorry. I promise." I turned and started down the L-hallway to the end, where my room was. Jerry followed. I tried to make small talk about what he liked to do outside of school or if he played basketball. He didn't reply. At least I would get him in the door.

I walked in and set my things down on a table. The room was stark, the walls made of large, yellowed cinder blocks that appeared to have been trying to pass for white at one time. The floors were badly chipped linoleum, with many tiles cracked or missing altogether. I thought to myself, *This isn't a far cry from what he had in lock-up!*

I turned around to invite Jerry to a seat. Jerry was squatting with his hands placed fingers inward on his thighs for support. His head was down, as if he were going to vomit. Then I realized what was happening. He wore his jeans low to begin with, but his boxers were now pulled down, as well. His bare thighs were visible between them and the hem of his XXL jersey. Something dropped to the floor.

Jerry was taking a dump.

Right there on my classroom floor and in front of me, Jerry was relieving himself. After leaving his last deposit, he unceremoniously hoisted his boxers back up and straightened his shirt. His face was all smug self-satisfaction. "That's what I thinka your *[expletive]* readin' class, *boy!*"

Now, this story could be used to illustrate a number of things I feel passionately about, and which are topics discussed elsewhere in this book. The fact that, regardless of our circumstances, we always have a choice. The benefits—and challenges—of choosing positivity over negativity. The idea that no one can *make* you mad. But here, I want to use it to talk about something else.

THE BEST ADVICE SO FAR:
Focus on the person not the problem.

In those few seconds, I had some decisions to make. I was certainly well within my rights to be furious with this kid! I could have called his probation officer on the spot and had him sent back to lock-up, or had him on the run until they found him. I could have called school security and had him removed. Heck, I could have called the police to come and arrest him, adding another charge to his record for exposing himself in public, and leaving him branded as a sex offender for the rest of his life. No one would have seen it as retaliation. Everyone would have understood and seen any of these choices as perfectly reasonable.

But I chose not to see the problem in front of me. I chose to see the person. The young man. The boy.

It was not important to me *what* he had done in that moment. It was more important to consider *why* he had done it. And that seemed obvious. This kid didn't hate me. He hated himself. He hated his failure. And he wasn't about to allow himself to be humiliated. Not anymore. And so he was willing to go to this extreme — seeing defecating in public as less shameful than how he had felt up until now in his life, than being branded as "stupid."

I spoke in an even tone, even kindly. "Well, Jerry, unfortunately, I'll have to give you a detention. You can leave for now. See you at 3:15."

He seemed defeated that I hadn't given him more of a reaction for all his effort. But he was still defiant. He began to shuffle toward the door. "I ain't coming to your *[expletive]* detention."

As he exited, I made sure he heard me: "Then you'll leave me with no choice but to call your probation officer. I'd hate to see that happen. You decide, though."

I did not report the incident. Other students who came down to see me all noticed the "present" Jerry had left. But I didn't give him away. I simply said, "Oh, yeah, one of the kids had an accident. I'm going to clean it up later." One kid, strangely, didn't even notice!

After school, I wondered whether I'd see Jerry. But I was prepared, in the event that he did show. 3:15— no Jerry. I waited.

At 3:25, Jerry slunk around the corner with his hands stuffed into his pockets and immediately noticed that his— statement—remained right where he had left it all those hours earlier. Beside it were gloves, a bucket with soap and water, disinfectant spray, bleach, paper towels and a red biohazard bag. I noticed the slightest hint of shame come across his face. Then it was gone. He straightened up. Hardened up. "I'm not cleaning that up," he informed me.

"I'm not asking you to," I said, moving toward the supplies and donning the gloves. I cleaned up the mess as quickly as I could, while being thorough. It took less than five minutes. Jerry didn't say anything. But he didn't walk away either.

"Your detention is over, Jerry. See you tomorrow

morning to give that reading stuff a shot. Have a good night."

The next morning, Jerry showed up to my classroom on time for his lesson. He said nothing. I didn't mention the episode the day before. "Hey, Jerry! Good morning. Glad to see you. Let the two weeks begin! Trust me on this—you're going to be reading before you know it."

Jerry sat down. But for the entire hour, he remained silent, staring off. This was a challenge, since teaching reading usually requires that the student read aloud. And we were working at the phonetic level. I had no idea if this was going to work. But I talked for the hour, giving myself the proper responses that Jerry should have been giving me. When the time was up, I thanked him for coming and told him I hoped to see him the next morning.

He came back. For two weeks he came back. And each day, he said nothing. Not a word. He slouched in his chair, with those half-closed eyes, looking sullen. Never looking at me. But he came. On the last day of the two-week period I'd challenged him with, I told him, "Well, Jerry, I told you that if you couldn't read better after two weeks, you could quit. The problem is...I don't *know* whether you can read better or not yet. But I'm going to leave the choice up to you. There are other students who need the help, and if you don't want to come tomorrow, I'll try to find someone else. But I *hope* you will come back. I like you. And I know you can do this."

To my surprise, Jerry came back the next day. And the next. At the end of the third week, I told him how proud I was of him for coming. He literally had not spoken to me in three weeks! But I cared a lot about this kid all the same.

Week four, Jerry showed up. Keep in mind that not *only* had Jerry come to my class all this time—it meant he had also *showed up to school every day for weeks*. By now, I was used to giving the instruction and the response for the hour. But today, mid-way through the lesson, Jerry spoke up. His voice sounded strange to me, not having heard it in all that time. He spoke loudly, almost belligerently. "*Why'd you clean up my sh*t?!*"

I remember how my eyes stung. All this time he'd been coming, thinking about this every day in silence. "I cleaned it up because I care about you. And because I've messed up many times in life, too, and been forgiven. And I wanted to do that for you."

He nodded, as if in acceptance. That was it.

I continued with my instruction. Only this time, he answered me. He still slouched, leaning on one fist with half-closed eyes. But he *answered*. What's more, he was *right*.

Four months later, Jerry was reading on a high school level. He was a different person. He had an insatiable desire to learn. He wanted to know everything. He began reading magazines. Then books. He wanted to know how to spell and write. And he was like a bodyguard to me, walking beside me proudly down halls, as if daring anyone else to mess with me.

Go back to Jerry's first day in my classroom. Consider what would have surely happened if I'd focused on the *what* instead of the *why*—on the problem instead of the person. Better yet, think of it in reverse. Look at what *did* happen because someone chose to see Jerry in terms of *why* and not *what*—as a *person* and not as a problem.

Now think about your own life. Do you tend to react to *what* the people around you do, without considering *why*? I'm convinced that, if we will choose to take the time to understand the *why,* the *what* will no longer bother us so much.

Questions for Reflection and Discussion:

APPENDIX page 367

CHAPTER 25

Expectations

I WAS VISITING MY BROTHER in North Carolina. It had been a long road trip, so the rest of my family there headed out to a flea market, leaving me to sleep in. When I finally woke up, the dog was whining, eager to get outdoors. I slid into some shorts and scuffed my sandals on. Opening the front door was like opening the door to an oven. It had to be 100 degrees.

Once outside, the schnauzer made fast work of the perimeter of the house and its bushes, then headed for the large central pin oak. As he clawed the grass, pulling against his leash, I stumbled, having nearly stepped on something. A toy? A mushroom? Whatever it was, something told me it shouldn't be trampled.

Upon closer inspection, I noticed three of these yet unidentified clumps, spread out over about a square foot of lawn. Quickly, I realized what they were. Baby birds. Frail and new. Feathers had only begun to form, and the pinkish, goose-bumped skin was clearly visible. The eyes were bulbous and closed in narrow slits. Were they alive?

I placed a finger gently under the beak of the nearest one. Immediately, its tiny neck stretched upward like a jack-in-the-box, its tiny yellow mouth opening instinctively. Its head wobbled precariously, as if it were a marionette on a string instead of a living thing. I touched the other two, and each responded in kind. They had survived the fall. But they would not survive much longer unaided.

I quickly let the dog finish his business and then brought him inside, returning to the tree to assess the situation. I looked up. About fifteen feet overhead, I saw the nest. It was out quite far, hanging at an angle—further along the branch than would bear my full weight, even if I could manage to climb the tree. Even the closest limbs were more than eight feet up the trunk.

My mom had always known what to do when it came to baby animals when we were growing up. I gave her a ring. No answer. She was still out at the flea market, and it didn't seem they would be home soon enough. I'd have to do something myself. And I'd have to do it now.

I found some gloves in my brother's garage, unsure of whether it were truth or urban myth that you can't touch baby birds or the mother will disown them. I'd rather not take chances. Still, gloves were great, but what was the plan here?

I decided that trying to return the birds to the nest was the best bet. My brother did not appear to have a ladder. But I gathered a few more things I might be able to use. I emptied plastic Easter eggs out of a canvas bag I'd found in my nephew's closet. I attached two long dog leashes to one another, thinking I may be able to use it as a hoist with the bag. Into the bag, I placed a shallow bowl.

Across the street, I saw a woman enter her house. Her garage door was open. I ran up to the house and rang the bell. She and her teenage daughter came to the door, looking skeptical.

"Hi, I'm staying with my brother across the street there," I began, "and some baby birds have fallen from the tree in front of his yard. I'm hoping to get them back into the nest, and I was wondering if you had a ladder I could borrow."

The mom paused, appraising. "Is this a joke?" she asked.

I smiled as disarmingly as I could. "No, no joke. You can come and see them if you like." I gestured toward the tree.

"This seems like one of those scary reality shows. You *look* like a nice guy, but you *could* be a murderer," she replied.

I was at a loss. "I'm... not a murderer," I said still smiling. "I promise. It's that yard right over there with the red jeep."

"Oh! The Boston fan!" she replied, seeming more at ease. "Yes, we have a ladder. It's only six feet. Will that be tall enough?"

"I think it just might!" I said. "Thank you so much."

In a few moments, she produced a red ladder and off I went.

I set the ladder up under the tree. It was immediately doubtful that it would, in fact, reach. But maybe it would get me close *enough*.

The first task would be to right the nest. I climbed up the ladder, gloves tucked into the back of my shorts. Even on the top rung of the ladder, I could just barely reach the nest. It would have to do. It certainly *was* near 100 degrees. I was sweating profusely.

Bits of bark rained down into my eyes, sticking to my

skin, as I grasped branches for stability. I had to squeeze between other branches to reach the one on which the damaged nest rested, pushing them out of the way using my back. It became painfully clear to me why this tree was called a *pin* oak. I knew I'd have scratches to deal with after this was done.

Stretching upward caused the ladder to wobble underneath. As it was, I'd had to place the base of the ladder so that it straddled where the birds dotted the lawn. If the ladder or I fell, some of them would certainly be crushed. I regained my footing and stretched again. I donned one of the gloves and then did my best to level and reform the nest, then pushed it deeper into the crook of the branch. Once it seemed it would hold, I backed down the ladder.

I tilted my head up to assess my work, shielding my eyes from the glaring sun. Looked solid. But that ladder was not going to be tall enough nor stable enough to complete the rest of the task before me.

Just then, I saw another neighbor boy come out of his door with some recyclables. I asked if his dad was home, and he said that, yes, he was. I knocked. The man spoke briefly with me and then extracted an eight-foot ladder from his garage and handed it to me over boxes and around vehicles. This one should do the trick!

I collapsed the red ladder and set up the new yellow one. Then I knelt on the ground and, using the gloves, I pulled grass from the lawn and placed it into the bowl. I figured this might make for an easier time scooping them up without hurting them, once I'd gotten the birds into the bowl. Finally, I picked up each bird with great care, placing them into the bowl. Of course, each touch, bump or move caused the jack-in-the-box reflex to kick in, punctuating the urgency to get them back into that nest where they might finally be fed again.

Climbing the ladder wearing gloves and carrying a bowl of birds was no easy task. The mother bird was back, hopping furiously from branch to branch, squawking stridently at me. I considered it a good sign. She wanted them.

Slowly, I made my way back to the top of the ladder, one hand holding the bowl of birds and one grasping overhead branches. This wouldn't work. I needed both hands to get the birds back into the nest. I couldn't just *dump* them in. I had to stand on the very top rung of the ladder to get high enough. This alone was daunting, and I was beyond hot by this time, as well. Sweat stung my eyes. I stooped down slowly, carefully, and set the bowl of birds on the ladder top next to my foot. So many things could go awry with this scene.

Still grasping the branch overhead, I managed to get one of the birds into my gloved fingers and then pulled myself upward, at the same time pulling the branch down a bit. I realized I was holding my breath. With painstaking care, I placed the first of the birds back into the nest.

Hope filled me, pushing me onward with renewed energy.

I stooped again, repeating the process for each of the remaining birds. The mother bird continued to watch with growing interest and mounting eagerness. At last, they were all back to safety. I'd done it!

As I stepped off the top of the ladder and made my way back down, I breathed a sigh of relief. Just as I got back to the ground, a car appeared around the bend, pulling into the driveway. Everyone was home.

I returned the ladders and then told everyone about the ordeal. My nephew and niece thought I was quite the hero. And I felt just a little like one, too.

Hours passed and I rechecked the lawn. As I opened the door, the mother bird flew off. I hoped it was for food. Perhaps *more* food. All of the birds remained in the nest. She hadn't discarded them.

At the same time, I realized that she very well *could* abandon them still. They might make it. But they might not. If they did, then my hard work and ingenuity would not have been in vain. But if they didn't?

This got me thinking about other things. Other sacrifices we make. Expectations. Calculations. Why we do what we do.

How many things in life do we engage in, only to feel disappointed or cheated—that we'd "wasted our time"— if they don't turn out as we had hoped? In fact, *is* our time and effort wasted if the desired outcome isn't achieved?

THE BEST ADVICE SO FAR:
Whatever you choose to do,
do it without expectations,
simply because you believe in doing it.

When I was in college, I did some interning with a youth program. That's where I met Brandon. At the time, Brandon was 12 years old. I don't think I ever saw him without a black, death metal T-shirt on. He smoked anything you could smoke. He drank—the hard stuff. He bragged about girls in their 20s who thought he was their age. His teeth were bad. His mouth was worse. He was a punk. A troublemaker. A real tough guy with a raging mullet, and a southern accent so thick you couldn't understand him at times, especially when he was upset and going off, which was often.

I loved that kid.

The week after meeting Brandon, he and his friend Mike were stuck for a ride, and I offered to give them a lift home. Both boys lived with grandparents who were their caretakers. I called each and, after explaining who I was, the grandparents had agreed to allow me to take the boys for ice cream before dropping them off. You'd have thought the two of them had died and gone to heaven. They clearly didn't go out much, at least not for normal kid stuff.

When I brought Mike home, I introduced myself to his grandparents. His grandmother was quiet, but his grandfather was a force to be reckoned with. He questioned me like a detective might. I actually appreciated it— appreciated that he cared enough to find out who was spending time with his grandson. After about twenty minutes, I had passed the test, and set out to get Brandon home.

On the short drive, Brandon said, "Can I tell you something?" It was clearly something big.

"Yeah, of course," I answered. "Anything."

"Well…" he began. We were already turning down his street. "Can we park out front for a minute?"

I was a little nervous about the delay already, having stayed so long at Mike's. And I didn't like the idea of sitting out front of Brandon's house in the car too long, being an unknown adult. But we parked. I turned toward him. He was looking down, fidgeting with his hands. I looked right at him. "Brandon, look at me." He looked at me sideways, eyes wide and his face drawing down as if he were ashamed. "Whatever it is you want to tell me, I want to let you know before you even say it that I'm going to like you just the same, and I will keep it to myself, OK?"

Recall that this was the second time I'd ever seen Brandon.

He exhaled and looked away again. "I know," he said quietly. "I know you will."

Brandon told me he'd been molested. Not once, but four times. And by different people. Most recently in a car. At gunpoint. Brandon explained what the man had made him do, and how he had managed during the act to open the car door and roll out and down a hill, escaping. This man was currently in prison, but would be released in another four years. Brandon was already afraid. "Why does this keep happening to me?" he said. "Am I sending out some kind of signal?" Tears streamed down freely. There was no "tough guy" in him as he sat there, drowning in shame and relief.

I bit my tongue. Literally. I was welling up, but I didn't want to let the tears actually fall, possibly making this worse for him. Here I was, a new guy showing up in Brandon's life. The last guy had lured kids to his place with free video games and pizza. I'd just taken him for free ice cream. What must he be thinking?

"Brandon—can you look at me one more time?" He looked. "I know you have absolutely *no* reason to believe me when I tell you this, but I'm going to tell you anyway,"

I said softly. "I am not going to do that to you. I am never going to do that."

"I know," he said. "I don't think that. I just... wanted you to know."

He looked away, and I put my hand on his shoulder quickly. He looked back. "And there is *nothing* wrong with you," I added. "Now, let's go meet your grandmother."

When I got Brandon to the door, he tried to convince me not to come in. "Granny'll be in bed. She's tired. Her nappy head is always in bed." I knew he felt uncomfortable about my coming in. Still, I wanted to set his grandmother's mind—and Brandon's—at ease. I convinced Brandon that it was OK to let me in, and that he didn't need to be embarrassed or make excuses.

When he opened the door, white smoke billowed out. If I hadn't known the smell of cigarette smoke, I'd honestly have thought there was a legitimate fire. Within the cloud, sparse and matted grey hair was just visible above the back of a dilapidated, brown leather recliner. A frail hand hung over the side holding the last of a cigarette over a crowded ashtray that spilled onto the floor. A televangelist was pacing and ranting on the small, tube television. "Brandon! Close that door!" came a crackling voice, before he'd even gotten a word out.

"Shut yo nappy head up, granny!" Brandon retorted. "I got Erik here!"

I quickly tried to ameliorate the situation, coming around to the side of the chair and squatting down. "Hi, Mrs. Clay. I'm Erik. Thanks for taking a chance and letting me take Brandon out. We had a great time. Now... I'm sure you have questions for me."

She turned her head slowly toward me, shaking, her lips working around missing teeth. She looked medicated. She appeared to be in her late 70s. I was to find years later that she'd only been in her 50s. "Hi," she said, sounding more like a grandmother now. "Thank you for taking Brandon home. I can't get him. I'm sick and I don't drive."

"That's no problem, Mrs. Clay. I'm happy to help and to spend time with Brandon. He's a great kid."

She looked over to where Brandon was sitting on a small couch. I felt as if she were trying to ask him something in that glance. *Did he…?*

I addressed her wordless concern. "Now, you don't know me at all, I realize. So I want to do everything I can to set your mind at ease. I'd like to give you some references of families whose kids I've known for years. And I'll also be happy to fill out a CORI form and have it mailed to you. And here's my phone number. And my mom's phone number. Sometimes, talking to someone's mom helps."

Looking back now, I probably overdid it. But then again, I was only nineteen.

She took the piece of paper from me and placed it beside the ashtray. She turned toward Brandon again.

"I told him," Brandon said bluntly.

His grandmother took it from there. "Brandon's had so many people hurt him."

"I know," I said gently. "I know. And that's why I want you to feel extra safe with me. So we'll get those references and CORI to you for starters."

We chatted a bit more, but then I had to go. Brandon walked me outside, closing the door behind him.

He thanked me over and over for the ride and the ice cream, and for talking to his grandmother and giving her all that information. I could tell there was something else though, something he wasn't saying. I made it easy for him. "You have something else on your mind. You've already told me the hard part tonight. So just... say it."

He kicked the step a couple of times, then just sort of fell forward into me. Instinctively, I hugged him. "I love you," he said, his voice muffled by my shoulder.

I hadn't expected that. My mind raced. How do you respond to that, especially given all of the circumstances here?

"I love you, too," was all I could come up with. And honestly, I felt it.

Brandon's grandmother *did* call my mom, and that *did* seem to set her mind at ease. Before long, I learned even more about Brandon.

His mother had gotten pregnant with him while overseas in the military. Germany. She'd called her mother, Mrs. Clay: "I'm pregnant. Either you take it or I'm having an abortion." She had delivered Brandon in the States. He was born with fetal alcohol syndrome. And that was the last time his mother had seen him, though she called from time to time, to ask her own mother to send money— money that was clearly not there to send. I was at the house during one of those calls. Brandon was arguing with his grandmother about something, as she was telling her daughter that she had no money. Again. Back and forth she went, between the phone and Brandon. "No, no I can't... Brandon, Brandon! Be *quiet!*... I told you, you know I'm on welfare... *I can't hear, now hush yo mouth!*"

Then she held out the phone to Brandon, announcing in a scolding tone, "Your *momma* wants to talk to you!"

Brandon's anger crystallized. He grabbed the phone. The woman on the line must have said something. Brandon replied, in colorful language, *"You can't [expletive] tell me what to do! And you ain't my [expletive] momma! You think you can just call here and [expletive] tell me what to do after you threatened to kill me or leave me in [expletive] Germany?"*

That was the first time Brandon had spoken to his mother.

I learned that he had two uncles who lived about an hour away. They never visited. But occasionally, Mrs. Clay would call one of them and ask them to come down and "belt" Brandon for something he'd done or said. And at an unannounced time, a man would show up and beat Brandon, throwing him into walls and leaving marks.

There was also Mrs. Clay's ex-husband, an alcoholic who lived on the streets. He would sometimes show up and steal something or threaten her to give him money or cigarettes. One night, Brandon called my dorm room, rasping in panicked whispers that I had to strain to understand. *"He's here. He's got granny. And a gun. I'm under the bed."*

I immediately called the police and then headed over. I'd get there first. To this day, I don't know what came over me, but I walked right in that front door. Louis had Mrs. Clay, and now Brandon, in a corner of her bedroom. I was completely calm. I felt strong. It was as if I were watching it all on television instead of living it. I walked quietly yet deliberately over to them and stood between the end of the gun and the two hostages. Louis was clearly beyond drunk. "Louis," I began in an even but forceful tone, "the police will be here any minute. So you can leave now, or you can go back to jail until you die." After a brief bluster of nonsense, he lowered the weapon and staggered quickly out the front door. The police arrived and arrested him as he exited. As soon as it was over, no part of me remained calm or collected. The whole of it swept over me like a taser and my knees buckled.

It all seemed a very odd life to me. Yet for Brandon, it was par for the course. Another day.

In the next couple of years, Mrs. Clay signed waivers to allow me to advocate for Brandon in her stead—at school, with police and in other legal matters. Brandon and I became very close. I saw him nearly every day for the rest of college, and he came to stay with me for a couple weeks on summer breaks. As graduation neared, I spent the entire year preparing Brandon, now 15, for my departure. For life afterward.

Graduation came and went. I moved back home. I talked to Brandon daily and did my best to advocate for him from a distance. I remember getting a call once from Patrick, another boy I knew from the area. Patrick was clearly drugged out. He and Brandon were at the home of an older woman, Dolores, who supplied them with drugs, alcohol and sex. I could hear Brandon screaming as if he were on fire in the background. I somehow managed to get Dolores on the line. My mother, a nurse, spoke authoritatively to her. "What did he take and how much, Dolores?" my mother asked clinically. I listened as best I could. "He's toxic, Dolores. You need to call 9-1-1. If you don't, he could die. And then it will be worse for you."

This is how things went, in that stretch of time after college. Then, a few months later, I got a call from one of the uncles. Mrs. Clay had had a stroke and was in the hospital. She'd asked if I would take custody of Brandon until she got well. Which might be never. I said I would. I was 22.

Brandon lived with me for nearly a year-and-a-half. Slowly, he adapted to structure. Very slowly. Between arson, running up phone bills, and continued struggles with drinking and drug use, I got a run for my money. At one point, in a rage because I'd followed through on a restriction, Brandon spit in my face and told me he hated me. He apologized in tears two days later. I adapted. He adapted. But he was never "fixed."

His second summer with me, I sent him back down to Virginia to visit with his grandmother, who was doing better by that time. That was the last time I saw Brandon.

He was implicated in a shooting, arrested and questioned without his grandmother's or my knowledge or consent. He was tried and sentenced to 50 years in prison, where he remains today. He was 16 when he went in.

So what does this have to do with baby birds?

A similar question arises in both cases here. If all of your efforts don't produce the desired result, is it worth it? Or is it just wasted time and energy?

I can't help but recall one of Carlotta's pieces of wisdom from earlier in this book: "If you're expecting someone else to make you happy, you never will be." It seems to apply to Brandon and to birds. To anything we choose to do in life. If we are expecting certain reactions or responses in order to make us happy, we will frequently be left disappointed.

If I help only because I expect praise or acknowledgement, then I'm setting myself up for disappointment. If I help for the joy of helping, then I am satisfied even if my help is unappreciated or unnoticed.

If I give, feeling entitled to something in return, then I may become bitter when that doesn't happen. If I give because I see a need and it is enough to have met it, then I am content in the giving.

If I save baby birds, somehow feeling that my efforts *deserve* to pay off, I may feel the world is cruel if the birds do not survive.

On that point, later that evening the mother bird threw the three babies from the nest again. And once more, by some miracle, they all survived. Two came down at once. Then a few hours later, in a storm, the third tumbled over the edge, wet and weak. As it turned out, a woman named Cherokee, who lived a few houses up, came by and offered to care for the birds until she could find a home for them. A wonderful turn of events, to be sure. But I knew, especially in the case of the last baby bird, that they still may not survive. And *yet,* I would do it all again. Why? Because I felt those baby birds deserved a chance. And because it kept my compassion limber. Strengthened my character.

In Brandon's case, it certainly had more of an emotional impact on me than did the birds. He was like my own son. Yet I have never felt that my time, energy or love were wasted. He was given an oasis in his otherwise tumultuous and harsh life, a respite during which he knew what it meant to be safe. To be loved unconditionally. That is never wasted. And in my own life—I couldn't begin to tell you in short order how those years with Brandon changed me for the better.

Whatever you choose to do in life, do it because you believe in doing it and for no other reason. Let go of expectations and demands. You will be the happier for it.

Questions for Reflection and Discussion:

APPENDIX page 369

CHAPTER 26

Humility

IT SEEMS TO ME that the idea of humility is most often greeted with groans of resistance. Or shame. In my opinion, it's gotten a bum rap. I suspect this has something to do with idiomatic speech:

> "Despite her *humble beginnings*, she overcame the odds and soared to stardom."

> "He had to *eat humble pie* when his accusations against his wife were proven to be untrue."   ·

> "I felt *humiliated* by your behavior at the party."

It seems the word "humility" in all its forms has somehow fallen into purely negative connotation. And so humility winds up feeling like a punishment—something forced upon us by life or by the jeering crowds who wish us the worst.

In fact, humility like most anything else, is a *choice*.

THE BEST ADVICE SO FAR:
Humility is a strength, not a weakness.

Let's suppose it's Thursday. I buy myself a delicious piece of gourmet cheesecake. My intent is not to eat it at the bakery or cafe, but rather to save it for tomorrow night, to celebrate having kept to my writing goals for the week. If I can finish one more chapter by then, I will take that cheesecake out of my fridge and enjoy my reward. Motivation.

It's tough, but I stay up into the early hours of Friday morning writing, staying focused. When I start to feel like I just can't finish, I go to the fridge and look at the cheesecake awaiting me. I pick it up. I smell it. Mmmm. I put it back and start typing.

Somehow, between everything else in my day Friday, I manage to finish that chapter. And it's a good one. Cheesecake, here I come!

The doorbell rings. It's one of the kids I mentor. The cheesecake will have to wait. I let him in and invite him to choose a can of soda from the several varieties I keep stocked in the fridge at all times (this has become a tradition among the kids entering my home, one which makes them feel instantly special and at ease). He calls out from the kitchen, "Woah! This cheesecake looks amazing! Is it leftovers?"

I have a choice to make.

But first, let me ask you, do I have a *right* to say no to this kid? Do I have a *right* to eat the cheesecake myself later? I mean, I bought it with my own money. What's more, I did the hard work of keeping to my writing goals so that I could fully enjoy the prize of eating it. But, even had I not met my goals, do I not have the right to withhold the cheesecake and keep it for myself?

Let's go a step further with it. Would it be consid-ered *unreasonable* for me to keep it for myself? Couldn't I simply say, "Hey, no, it's not leftovers. I bought it to motivate myself to keep writing this week. And I did write a lot! So, I'm gonna have it a little later to celebrate." Perfectly understandable, is it not?

The truth is, I do in fact have every *right* to the cheesecake. And it would be perfectly *reasonable* for me to exercise that right.

I'd like to suggest that humility be defined this way: "fully realizing my right to something, and then willfully giving up that right in order to honor another person."

Give that proposed definition a minute to sink in.

If this is how we define "humility," is it coming from a position of weakness or strength?

Now, true humility knows its rights. But it does not proclaim them. Imagine that I say to the teen, "Well, you know, I bought that cheesecake for myself as a reward, and I really wanted to enjoy it later. But, yes, you can have it." While I may still be giving away the cheesecake, I've muddied things by proclaiming my right to it. In some ways, I've not really given up my rights to it. I've sort of transferred them in a way that may make my friend feel as if he "owes" me if he eats it. Even if my payoff is that I want the teen to think I'm a better person because of what I'm doing, I've traded my rights to the cheesecake for the right to his thanks or respect. I haven't honored him so much as I've honored myself for being such a good person.

Perhaps I feel that I *must* give up my right to the cheesecake in order to be liked. Or that, because someone else asked, I no longer *deserve (i.e., have a right)* to keep the cheesecake for myself. Here, I am not giving something away willfully. I am acting in fear that I will lose love or affection. Or I believe that my right has somehow been *taken* from me by someone more worthy. I would proffer that neither of these is real humility. Here, I am not so much honoring someone else as *dishonoring* myself.

With true humility, I *know* my rights. And I know that I *can claim them*. Then, fully realizing this, I *choose* to forgo my rights, because I see the value in someone else, and because I want to honor them by giving them what was rightfully mine to claim. So, I say to my young friend, "You know what? I would love for you to eat that cheesecake. Have at it!"

And then I sit back and truly enjoy *his* enjoyment of "my right" to the cheesecake.

Just for the record, I don't need to wait for this guy to notice the cheesecake. Maybe, during the course of chatting with him, I realize that he is feeling down. Tarnished. Un-special. Imagine the impact if I remember my cheesecake and set aside my right to it, seeing it as a tool to help give this kid a sense of his value in the world. He is worth having my special cheesecake! I am no less worthwhile, but I'm not struggling with that at the moment. He is. So I make that choice.

Consider giving humility its good name back. Imagine it as polished steel rather than a wet sponge. Color it cobalt blue in your mind, instead of pale yellow. And then put it into practice—not as a punishment, but as a privilege.

Questions for Reflection and Discussion:

APPENDIX page 371

CHAPTER 27

Awkwardness

YOU JOSTLE THE COOING BABY up over your head, making ridiculous faces and jabbering nonsense at him. He really seems to think you're a miracle of entertainment, when suddenly, he regurgitates vast amounts of sour formula onto your face.

You leave a conversation where you thought you were dead sexy, only to notice, in adjusting your rearview mirror, that there is an unsightly, fluttering flake hanging from your nostril.

Your spoon somehow flies onto a nearby table at a restaurant. The cat gets caught in your hair. Life is a string of awkward moments.

Awkwardness is a hard emotion to describe. Go ahead. Try it. Awkwardness is icky. Awkwardness is blecht [insert head-to-toe shudder here]. Awkwardness is just… well… awkward. And if it's that hard to describe what awkwardness feels like, how the heck do we deal with awkward situations and make that awkward feeling go away?

THE BEST ADVICE SO FAR:
Putting awkwardness out there on the table by calling it what it is immediately takes most of the awkwardness out of it.

"Wait!" you protest. "You seriously want me to *TALK* about the awkward thing? Blecht!" [Re-insert aforementioned head-to-toe shudder here.] This seems counterintuitive. Illogical even. But, in actuality, awkwardness is born when everyone knows something happened but no one will mention it. It morphs and becomes an ever-growing, hideous monster as people begin to wonder what everyone else is thinking about the situation. Or what everyone else is thinking about what I'm thinking. Mentioning the awkward thing is a lot like throwing water on the Wicked Witch of the West. It melts away before your very eyes.

So, let's say that Joe likes Jane. Joe and Jane went on a few dates and it seemed they were having a grand time. Joe kissed Jane at the end of date six. Jane stopped returning Joe's calls. Jane is now going out with Lloyd. Yes, I said Lloyd. And now Joe has been invited to the birthday party of Sam, who is a mutual friend of Jane's. Awkwardness takes over. Joe's thought process looks something like this:

"I really liked Jane. Then she just stopped calling. Was it because I kissed her? Did she ever even like me at all? Did I just think we were having fun, while she was hating every minute we were together? Did I have an unsightly, fluttering flake that I didn't know about hanging from my nostril? And now… Lloyd! I mean, really—Lloyd? Well, doesn't this just stink! Now I can't go to Sam's party. And then Sam is going to be mad at me. But really, what choice do I have? I haven't talked to Jane in months, and she'll be there with—Lloyd!—and she probably told everyone I kissed her and that it was awful and that I was boring. And there I'll be at the party, and the record will scratch (even though there aren't records anymore), and it will be silent, and everyone at the party will stop and stare at me and start laughing in slow motion."

OK, Joe. Take a deep breath. Here's what you do.

Go to the party, for Pete's sake (I have it on good authority that Pete does not know Jane, so it is all right to do it for his sake). Talk with a few friends. If Jane sees you from across a room, wave cordially, but do not make a bee line for Jane. Or away from her. Just continue doing whatever it was you were doing. Talking with another friend. Staring at the food table.

At some point, casually make your way over to Jane (whether she is standing with Lloyd or not). Smile and say, "Hi, Lloyd. Hi, Jane. You know, I have to be honest. It's a little awkward seeing you here. At one point, I wasn't sure if I should come. But I'm glad I decided to be here for Sam's birthday. Hope it's not too weird for you."

Period. Stop talking. You have put the awkward thing on the table. There is no need to ask every question your paranoid mind wondered during the last three months, Joe.

Very quickly, you should find yourself breathing at a slower pace and feeling the tension go out of your shoulders.

Jane will likely have a short response such as,

"Yeah, it's a little weird. But I'm glad I came, too."

Maybe she'll say less. Or, if she's really, really mean—and some girls are—maybe she will say something dreadful like, "I can't believe you're stalking me! Lloyd and I are going out now, you know. And, by the way, he is a *way* better kisser than you."

Hey, it's possible, Joe. Let's not pretend you hadn't imagined she might say it.

But that's OK! You are armed with your great new advice! You see, if Jane decides to go postal on you at the party—it's just another awkward moment. And you will put it right back on the table: "Wow, that's awkward, Jane. I'm not sure what to say about that, so I'm going to go grab a cookie now. Enjoy the party." You nod. "Lloyd."

Believe it or not, it's that simple. Awkwardness will have no power over you if you can master this simple strategy. And you will be the envy of the other party-goers, with your amazingly cool, calm and debonair approach to awkward situations.

Questions for Reflection and Discussion:

APPENDIX page 373

CHAPTER 28

Apologies

A SHOCKING AMOUNT of English language usage is idiomatic.

I can't help but smirk (and cringe) at the current usage of "literally" to mean "figuratively," as in "I'm literally burning up" to mean "I'm hot." Or "I literally died when I heard the news" to mean that one is merely somewhat surprised by it.

Even standard fare such as "I have to go to the bathroom" isn't as straightforward as it may seem at first. Do you *have* anything at all, in the sense of possession, when you say this? I suppose so, but it certainly isn't what we mean, nor is it anything we would probably like to expound upon. Are we merely *going to* the bathroom— walking there and then walking back? Again, this is just an avoidance of the not-so-polite facts of the matter. And does the *bathroom* in every case even contain a bath? Yet it's a good deal better than going the literal route by saying, "I must urinate into the toilet now."

Idiomatic usage is perhaps the clearest earmark of a proficient speaker, and is both fascinating and necessary. But in many cases (such as the figurative use of "literally"), I fear we've begun to invite proverbial boys to cry wolf. In short, we're making it too easy to not mean what we say.

I'm one of those people who finds myself quoting lines from movies often. It's rarely the "big lines" that stand out to me. I'm more fascinated by the clever tidbits that tend to go largely unnoticed by the masses. In one such movie scene, a brother and sister, on in years, mistakenly wind up with an orphan girl named Anne in their home, having expected to be getting a boy instead. An outspoken neighbor barges in to see what all of this is about. She begins to chastise her friend about the new arrival in third person, as if the girl is not even there. "She's awfully skinny and homely, Marilla. She's certainly nothing to look at. And, her hair!" she gasps in shock. "It's as red as carrots!"

This last twit about the hair is more than the fiery Anne can bear in silence. Eyes bulging, she stomps forward, insolently. "Carrots! How would you like it if someone said that you were *fat*… and *ugly*… and a *sour old gossip*!"

The neighbor storms off, outraged, putting the matron of the house in a precarious situation, which results in an ultimatum: apologize to the neighbor woman… or go straight back to the orphanage. Anne is resolute that she will not apologize. But after some cajoling from Matthew, Marilla's meek and kindly brother, she concedes.

Anne and Marilla make the trek over to the neighbor's porch. Anne kneels down before the neighbor, hands clenched together imploringly. She delivers what proves to be quite a dramatic and self-deprecating apology. As the conclusion approaches, Anne offers, "What you said about me is true. I am skinny. And ugly. And my hair is red." After a brief pause, the next line comes out all in a rush. "What I said about you is true, too, only I shouldn't have said it."

I always laugh at this. After all the rhetoric and theatrics, she finally gets around to saying what she really means. How refreshing.

From the time children are able to utter the words, we make them say they are sorry:

"Tell Timmy you're sorry for throwing the block at his face!"

"Tell grandma you're sorry for pinching her!"

"Tell the cat you're sorry for pulling its tail!"

Of course, these mandates are given with a scowl of disapproval and a stern tone that implies "…or else." And so, in the name of proper manners and with the best of intentions, we teach our tots to say what they do not mean. Over time, the word "sorry" begins to collect other meanings:

"Stop being mad at me."

"Do what I want you to do."

"Don't leave me."

As wonderful and rich as our language is, I recommend revitalizing the words "I'm sorry" by reserving them for times when you mean precisely that.

THE BEST ADVICE SO FAR:
Apologize less and mean it more.

Secondary meanings for "I'm sorry" are common among both people users and people pleasers alike. The former mean "let me take advantage of you one more time," while the latter mean "please don't stop liking me." Both overuse the phrase. Neither is communicating honestly.

Some good people argue that it would be best to apologize even when you do not believe you are in the wrong, for the sake of "being the bigger person" and keeping the peace. In this case, "I'm sorry" would seem to mean "I care about you, and I'm willing to take the hit so we can get along." I've changed my views on many things over the years. This is one area in which I have not. I still believe that an apology should only be made with careful consideration, after some honest self-reflection, and under specific circumstance. This is the only way for the words to reflect true depth of meaning.

These are the guidelines I follow when it comes to making apologies:

Only apologize when I accept responsibility for a wrong done (whether known to the other person or not).

Consider how my actions were or may have been hurtful and express this.

Name the offense specifically when apologizing.

Verbally commit to a change of action or attitude for the next time a similar situation arises.

Ask the other person to forgive me.

Let's see how this might look when applied to a few different situations.

A big advertising campaign is due to be presented Friday, but your part is done and submitted plenty ahead of time. To celebrate, you make plans to have dinner out with your wife Thursday night.

Midday Thursday, you are informed that another department made some significant improvements and changes to the campaign, which will now necessitate that your contributions be entirely reworked. It's going to be a late night. You call your wife to cancel dinner plans. Do you apologize?

If we hold it up to the guidelines I suggest above, we would start by asking, "Do I accept responsibility for a wrong done here?" Given these circumstances, I would say no. Likewise, we cannot name the specific offense for which we are taking responsibility, nor can we commit to doing anything differently should a similar situation occur in the future. So, in this case, an apology is not what is called for. I won't stand on a hill and shout that "I'm sorry, honey, I have to cancel our plans tonight" is the worst thing you could say. Yet I still firmly believe that, in the scope of life, apologies will mean more if we make them less.

What might we say in this case, then? We can certainly empathize with how this change might be hurtful or disappointing, without taking responsibility for having caused that hurt or disappointment: "I know it stinks, honey. We both were really looking forward to our date. Tomorrow, one way or another, this presentation will be over. Why don't we go then?"

New scene. Your newborn brother has been wailing for more than an hour, while your frustrated mother has tried to sooth him and get him to sleep. Finally, he's drifted off and your mom has laid him in his crib. You're now helping your mom wash the pots and pans from dinner. She passes you a wet pan to dry, and it slips from your hands, clanging to the floor. A high-pitched shriek emanates from the baby's room, and your mother stares at the ceiling, exasperated. Do you apologize?

It's clear that the clanging pan woke the baby, and you were the last one to touch it. However, it was not a wrong. The fact that it happened to wake the baby does not somehow make it one. Accidents happen. But let's say that you were attempting to use the guidelines from this chapter and decided, "Well, I dropped it, so I'll take responsibility." Certainly, we can see how the "offense" negatively affected the baby and mom. It would seem a little weird to specifically name the offense ("I dropped the pan"), but I suppose we could do that, too. What about a plan of action for the next time? Will being more careful prevent wet items from slipping in the future? Were you truly not being careful? Or was it just "one of those things"? I think this is where the need for an apology gets ruled out here.

So, what could you say instead? Try, "Oh no! I feel awful! You worked so hard to get him to sleep. Do you want me to finish the dishes? Or would you rather have me try to get him back to sleep?"

One more scenario. Your friend Dave shared something with you in strict confidence. Later, your friend Shawn asks what's up with Dave, because he's noticed that Dave has been acting funny. You say to Shawn, "Dave told me what's up and asked me not to tell anyone. If I tell you, you have to *promise* me that you will keep it to yourself." Shawn promises, of course (who doesn't, when faced with the prospect of getting good dirt?), and you tell him.

The next day, Dave texts you:

thx 4 keeping

my personal life

to urself loser

You text him back—"**???**"—and receive Dave's reply:

figure it out

Do you apologize?

There is no question that you were in the wrong here. And it really doesn't matter how Dave found out. So going to Shawn and trying to track who said what to whom isn't the point. You were wrong. Broken trust is certainly hurtful to a relationship. You know exactly what you did and when. Can you sincerely commit to a change of action in the future? Can you ask Dave to forgive you? If so, then your apology may sound like this:

"Hey, Dave. I screwed up. You asked me to keep

that information to myself… and I didn't. I told Shawn. That was wrong. Now I've embarrassed you and damaged your trust in me. I'm really sorry. I will understand if you don't want to confide in me again; but if you do, I will prove that I can keep my mouth shut. Will you forgive me?"

A few more thoughts on apologies.

Whenever possible, apologize in person, not through email, text or relaying a message through another person. Those are, for the most part, copouts. Have the character and decency to feel uncomfortable for a few minutes and deliver the apology face to face.

Apologies do not contain an "if." It does not matter "if" the other person is sorry, too, even if you were both wrong. Being truly sorry means that you realize what *you* did was wrong, regardless of whether anyone else was wrong or willing to admit the same.

In a different sense of "if," many people tend to phrase apologies as, "I'm sorry *if* you were offended, but…" This is not an apology. It is actually nothing more than a clever rewording of "You should be sorry for being so sensitive; it's a wonder that anyone can speak to you at all." And that is how it is generally received. Remember that the first rule of thumb here is an acceptance of your *own* wrongdoing, not someone else's actions or reactions to what you did. In cases where you truly do not feel you were wrong, but feel the urge to apologize, try something like this instead: "I see how hurt you are. Please believe that it was not my intention to hurt you. Had I known it would affect you this way, I would have done it differently. I didn't know at the time, but I do now."

Even when you do genuinely apologize, the other person may or may not express forgiveness for you at that time. They may never forgive you. They may or may not trust you again. An apology is not a means to an end, given in order to regain your relational standing or to get someone to stop being angry with you. It is a sincere realization and admission that you were wrong, that you hurt someone, and that you intend to change.

At the very least, carefully considering and redefining "I'm sorry" will cause your apologies to mean something again.

Questions for Reflection and Discussion:

APPENDIX page 375

CHAPTER 29

Saying No

I USED TO HAVE A HARD TIME saying no to people. It didn't matter how many plates I had spinning at the time, if someone held another plate out and asked, "Gee, could you spin my plate, too?" I felt obliged to spin it along with the others. When I was younger, I think I told myself that saying yes was the same thing as being nice. Nice people say yes. Mean people say no. People like nice people. I like people to like me.

At some point along the way, however, I began to realize that I often had an awful lot of anxiety for such a "nice" person . Saying yes often made me actually *feel* mean. Resentful. Bitter. Call it what you will, I wasn't happy, just worn out.

It was not easy to break my addiction to yes. But I slowly and surely began to add "no" to my vocabulary. The problem was that I tried my best to make no sound like yes, or at least *feel* like yes. I did this by way of explaining to a painful degree exactly *why* I was saying no. I would explain in detail my schedule of every other obligation, broken down into days and hours. I would compliment and affirm that I liked the person who was holding out the current plate, and assure them that, under other circumstances,

I would, of course, gladly spin theirs. I would tell them how much I hated saying no, and how it had been a life-long struggle, and how my high school English teacher had tried to force me say yes to a recitation in a poetry competition in which I was already entered in ten other events, and how I was needing to say no sometimes now for my own well-being.

In my mind, all of this explanation somehow tricked people into feeling like I was a yes kind of guy, even when I was saying no. In my mind, people cared deeply to hear all the details of my no. In my mind, they walked away probably even glad I had said no, because they felt they now knew me better for it. In my mind, I was keeping the universe in balance.

In reality, I was still completely stressed out after saying no. *Did I cover all the bases? Are they mad at me? Was my overly detailed explanation suspect?*

One Christmas, many years back, my friend Dib gave me a wonderful book. In that book was a gem of advice that I have both practiced and passed along countless times since:

THE BEST ADVICE SO FAR:
"No" is a complete answer.

Somehow, the book made it seem both simple and logical that I could actually just say no without any further explanation necessary. Of course, there was a certain finesse that could be added to the starkness of no:

"I'm sorry, I won't be able to help."

"I'm afraid I can't."

"I'm going to have to pass on this one."

Add a pleasant smile, and that's it. Done. End of story. Interestingly enough, this advice appeared not in a book about being assertive, but in a book about etiquette, implying that not only is this response complete in itself, it is also sufficiently polite.

Notice the absence even of "I'm busy" or "My schedule is crazy right now." The truth is, regardless of what we might imagine, people generally accept a simple no as enough information.

What's more, even in the case of that really pushy person, the to-the-point approach of just saying no leaves precious little room for emotional manipulation or finding loopholes in the story. It puts the onus on the other person to have to say, "Well, why the heck not?" And most people realize that this, ironically, is *not* good etiquette.

All the time I saved foregoing tedious explanations, I was able to invest in figuring out why I felt the need to say yes or to have people always like me in the first place. The end result is that I no longer become anxious when people ask me to do something. I don't have to wonder what I will say. It's either, "Yes, I can" or a friendly "No, I'm sorry, I can't." I like me better. I like life better. And people seem to like me just as much as in the dark days of my addiction to yes and over-explanation of no.

Two quick exceptions should be noted.

If your no started out as yes, a bit more in the way of an explanation may be warranted (e.g., "I don't know how I managed to do it, but I overbooked. Could we reschedule?"). But the rule still applies—keep your revised no short and to the point.

If you are saying no to a close friend, feel free to share in more detail. Since people define "close friend" differently, I'll share what it means to me in the context of saying no. A close friend is someone from whom you feel no pressure anyway when saying no. In other words, a close friend is someone who makes it easy for you to say no. However, this kind of friend is also completely fine with the short form of no! So the details of your *no* only need be shared if it makes for a good story that induces plenty of laughter. Or that must-share-with-close-friend sort of cringing feeling.

Questions for Reflection and Discussion:

APPENDIX page 377

CHAPTER 30

Avoidance

Y OU COULD HAVE THE PATIENCE of Job. You could be helpful, kind and polite. You could be a good listener. You could be the nicest person in the world. And there are still going to be people you'd rather avoid.

You know what I'm talking about. You're halfway down the aisle at the supermarket, and there they are. They've just rounded the corner and haven't seen you yet. Or maybe they have. What do you do?

You leave, of course. You hold your breath, turn your shopping cart around, murmur apologetically to a clerk something about not feeling well. And you hightail it out of there.

Maybe for you, it's perpetually ignoring calls, texts or emails from someone. Or maybe you don't attend a party or family gathering because this person will be there.

Putting on the shades. Pulling up the hood. Hanging your hair in front of your face. Flat out bolting. I refer to all of these tactics as *ducking*. I know them well, because I used to do them a lot. And why not, really? If it's going to save you some stress, isn't it worth avoiding certain people? Preferring flight over fight, and all that?

Sounds good. I used to tell myself the same thing. But I've found that ducking as a lifestyle actually creates its own stress, even when you're not ducking in the moment.

THE BEST ADVICE SO FAR:
Decide never to duck around corners in life.

When it comes to people we duck from, they don't just cease to exist when they are not in our immediate space. We either think about them too much—replaying that last argument, imagining what we *should* have said, ruminating on the audacity of how they treated us—or we expend considerable effort trying *not* to think of them. And that is a whole lot like trying not to think of the red fox (go ahead and try it: whatever you do, *don't* think about a red fox). Or trying to win "The Game" (the one where, if you think about "The Game," you lose). The point is, you can't win. And all of this is using up mental and emotional space.

Now, there are certainly people that we'd like to avoid and whom we *don't* think about in between. The relative who corners the unwary at family picnics and talks their ear off, prattling on about nothing. The too-loud laugher who invades your personal space, reducing it to an inch or two. The guy whose face is tacked up on the bulletin board at the post office. I'm not talking about these people. I'm talking about people with whom we have a history. The estranged brother. The friend who betrayed you. The boss who fired you or the co-worker who spread lies about you. The ex. Or the ex's new love interest.

I've come to the conclusion that there are essentially three reasons why we might duck from someone:

1. We did something wrong to them (or someone they love) and have not made it right.

2. They did something wrong to us (or someone we love) and have not made it right.

3. Something about our history together just makes it awkward to see them.

Let's take a look at each.

If we are ducking because we've wronged or hurt someone, there's a fairly straightforward solution: make it right. Apologize without equivocation or excuse. While this may make you sweat to even think about it, it's fairly simple to do, at least in the mechanics of it. Think about it like getting a shot at the doctor's. It's a few moments of pain. Then you're all better. You can even go buy yourself a lollipop afterward, if you like. But do it. (See the previous chapter "Apologies.")

Unloading this kind of baggage is completely within your control. It's a choice. And the benefits to your peace of mind—not to mention your character—are astounding. Imagine that sleeping in an 80-degree room in the summer time is the coolest you've ever known. You've adapted. But then you suddenly experience bedtime at 70 degrees. Ahhh. You'll never want to go back to the 80-degrees you thought was the best it gets.

While you have 100% control over the choice to apologize, you have 0% control over the reaction you will get. So don't let it be about that. Keep it simple and sincere. Then let the cards fall where they may. Most often, people will accept a sincere apology. Some may pontificate about how you darned-well *ought* to be apologizing. A few may greet your apology with open disdain and tell you that it just isn't good enough. Whatever the case, stand there and take it. Say little beyond what you came to say. Of course, if there is some actual damage you've done, do your best to right it. And that's it. There is no more need to duck from this person. If you see them in the future, hold your head high, smile pleasantly and say hi, then go about your business, knowing you've set things right as far as was within your power.

In the case of the person who has hurt you or someone you love, they took control in the past when they hurt you. But every time you avoid them—and even in holding onto the bitterness you feel toward them—you are *giving* them the power. Over and over. Take it back. First, I recommend being sure they know that there is a problem. Have you at some point let this person know of the offense and how it affected you? Keep in mind that your perception may be off, and listen. But if you've done this, the person knows they have wronged you, and they just don't care, then there's no need to have continued conversation about it. When you see them, you don't need to stare them down, mentally reminding them of what a dirty so-and-so they are. By all appearances, passing this person in the aisle at the supermarket should appear much like passing a stranger in a country whose native language you do not know well. Hold your head high. Smile and nod politely. And move on.

Obviously, there is more to dealing with hurt and pain from the past than can be covered here. But I highly recommend taking measures to free yourself from it. Again, every day that the pain continues to be part of your life is another day you give away. A counselor could be helpful, or talking openly with a trusted friend. I know one brave young woman who wrote a letter to her sexually abusive step brother, telling him in her own words how much he hurt her. She ended the letter telling him, at least in words for the time being, "I forgive you. And now I'm moving on." But in live situations, don't duck. If you have done nothing wrong, remind yourself of that and decide that you will not allow this person to alter your life in the present.

Where a history with someone is simply awkward, and not a matter of right and wrong, I am a big fan of just putting the awkwardness out there on the table: "Hi. It's a little weird running into you, but hey, whatever, right?" While this may seem counterintuitive, simply mentioning that a situation is awkward takes most of the awkwardness out of it immediately (see the previous chapter "Awkwardness.")

I decided many years back that I would not duck around corners ever again. It's not always easy. But if you stick to it, almost formulaically, the rewards in terms of freedom and peace of mind will be enormous.

Questions for Reflection and Discussion:

APPENDIX page 379

CHAPTER 31

Bowing Out

I WAS INSPIRED WITH THE IDEA to write this book one June. By July, I'd decided on a title and sat down facing a blank page, ready to begin writing the first chapter. And that blank page looked wonderful to me. I was filled with the feeling I used to get as a boy, going back-to-school shopping for supplies. There was something magical about picking out a sturdy notebook with unbent spiral wiring and clean manila dividers, or a ring-binder with metal tabs that opened the clasps with a satisfying *click* when pressed. About browsing the shelves for new crayons (particularly the large variety box with the built-in sharpener). And about a tightly shrink-wrapped package of ruled white paper. I can feel the weight of it in my hands even now. I want to bend it and see the plastic stretch and become shiny. I love to look at the holes in the margin, all still perfectly lined up. I imagine getting it home and feeling the exhilaration of pulling the package until it's taut, pressing my thumbnail in until it pops, and running it along the top ridge, splitting it open. I smell the pulp and ink. It smells like hope and possibility.

That's how I felt in July as I began to write. And that first chapter poured out, furious and inspired. After writing it, I read it over. I laughed at all the right parts. I believed it. I sent it to a couple of friends and read it to my mother. I read it to a group of teens. And they laughed at all the right parts. We had meaningful discussions about the advice the chapter held. One friend even asked if he could pass it on to a couple of other people he thought could use the advice at the time. I was encouraged and excited. I had momentum. I wrote daily—sometimes completing two chapters in a single day—with the goal of finishing the entire book in three months.

It was now May, nearly a year later. I had not written since before Christmas. Five months with not a word.

What happened? What took that initial wind out of my sails and left me stranded in a sea of stagnation?

The answer to that question lies somewhere between advice elsewhere in this book, on saying no and on remembering that we always have a choice. It's advice I've given many times, and yet which I forgot to apply myself during these past months. And forgetting resulted in setbacks to both my goals and my overall sense of wellbeing. Because of the personal impact, I've become convinced that it deserves its own chapter—a chapter I had not planned to include in this book until now.

THE BEST ADVICE SO FAR:
Sometimes, it's better to run from a beast than to try to tame it.

Yes, I know. That makes no sense in light of what I said above. But it will.

Technically, I should have written it in caps—

BEAST—because, while I'm using it metaphorically, I'm also using it as an acronym:

Big Energy-Absorbing Stupid Thing

I trust however, for the sake of flow, that you won't be too hard on me if I use the less assaulting lower-case version.

We all have beasts in our life.

We choose them.

We invite them in.

Most often, a beast is not a grunting rhino when we first encounter it. We do not throw our doors open to a pacing lion, licking its chops, and say "Come on in, beast! Have the run of the place!" Usually, what we invite in is a seemingly docile, harmless, even helpless little thing. But it grows. Little by little, it grows. And it gets ornery. And hungry. It breaks things and eats our treats without asking. It keeps us up at night. And soon we find ourselves tiptoeing gingerly around the edges of our own lives, hoping not to rile the beast.

A beast could be a book club gone bad. At first, we joined to be more social or because a friend urged us to go. The people there are polite and laugh and drink tea. We're something of a celebrity as the new member. Our friend says all kinds of wonderful things by way of introduction. But then, somewhere along the line, it changes. We don't keep up with the next book and people get snippy. We share an opinion that others disagree with, and they begin to turn their shoulder to us at future meetings, acknowledging us only with a tight-lipped grin and eyes half closed in disdain. The friend who invited us begins missing two times out of three.

A beast could be a relationship. We have some laughs over old times with a friend from high school with whom we've recently reunited. But soon, she is showing up to dinner uninvited. Wanting to do lunch every week. Calling daily. Feeling jilted when we decline plans, or don't reply to texts within an allotted time. Sending sullen emails.

A beast could be a town sports league. A committee. Vacation plans. A church.

Whatever it is, it starts innocently enough. But soon, it grows into that Big Energy-Absorbing Stupid Thing— that beast that saps our vitality and creativity, causes dread and headaches, and drains the color out of our days.

Yet, so often, what do we do? We stick with it. We try to tame it, to make it manageable. We invest all kinds of time and energy, and conversations with the good people in our lives, into trying to "fix it." We forget that, even though we invited it in at first, we still have a choice. We can choose to open the door and kick the beast out. We can shut the door. Right the furniture and clean up the mess.

We can move forward without it.

It's rarely easy. We'll have to navigate through the awkward conversations and the guilt trips. We may even have to hurdle our own emotions in feeling that we are quitting or letting people down who "needed us." But then…

Then we start living again.

I realized I had lost track of my own beast. I loved it when it was tiny and new and fluffy. If I'm honest, I knew it was growing. Taking up more space inside. Growling at me a lot more often. But I kept trying to tame it, to see it as it was when it was small and innocent. Only it wasn't small and innocent any longer.

Putting the beast out was messy. But it was neither as long nor as painful a process as I'd imagined it would be. And the day after I locked the door behind it, I woke up feeling fifteen years younger. I'd been telling friends and family for a while that I just felt old. Tired. Like I wasn't getting enough sleep. Like even coffee had no effect. But that very next day after I said goodbye to the beast, it was as if I'd come up for air after being held underwater against my will. The sun seemed brighter. I played the piano for the first time in months. I set into some French lessons, remembering my trip to Paris last October and feeling my heart quicken at the thought of the next visit. I laughed. People who knew me noticed the change instantly. "You seem—great!" they exclaimed.

And I began writing this chapter.

Understand that, when I talk about evicting beasts, I am not advocating for walking out of a marriage when it becomes more difficult, or throwing your rebellious adolescent to the curb with a knapsack and a "nice knowing you." I am talking about remembering that many of the things which we allow to negatively impact our lives are voluntary. Extras.

If there is a beast in your life, remember that you are not a victim. It cannot force you to remain its prisoner even a day longer.

You *can* get back to enjoying your life.

You have a choice.

Questions for Reflection and Discussion:

APPENDIX page 381

CHAPTER 32

Condolences

Y EARS BACK, a friend of mine lost her husband suddenly. One minute, he had been painting the house, the next he had taken a nap and died of a heart attack. Unexpected and devastating.

Afterward, she reflected with me about goings-on at the wake. Even in her grief, she managed to maintain her sense of wry humor as she recounted story after story of well-meaning people who had said precisely the wrong thing to her.

"I guess God needed him more."

"I know it's hard, but isn't it wonderful that he's with the Lord now?"

The most bizarre account was of a woman who, as she came through the receiving line, had actually said to my friend, a nurse, "Listen, while I have you, could I just ask a quick question? I need to have a hysterectomy soon. Which procedure do you recommend?"

My friend's responses to each of these:

"What could God possibly need from my husband that I don't need more?"

"Given a choice between him being around the corner at the store and being with the Lord, I'd choose option A."

And to the baffling medical question, she could only smile wanly and say, "I'm sorry, that's my husband there in the casket. Now's not the best time."

Death itself is awkward. It's just part of the package. And a wide range of not-so-helpful responses often spring forth out of that awkwardness.

THE BEST ADVICE SO FAR:
When it comes to loss, keep it sincere and simple.

I'm a big fan of the idea that the tried-and-true standbys are still the best:

"I'm sorry for your loss."

"I'm here if you need me."

"Please let me know if I can help in any way."

If you can get by with a hug and a warm, supportive smile, better still.

Remember that grief and loss are not restricted to funeral homes. Life pain takes many forms, from tragedy and death, to illness and injury, to relational strain and divorce. In order to better understand how to respond to these situations, here are some things *not* to do.

1. Don't try to fix it.

Many times, we feel a sort of burden to have some magical "right thing" to say that will cheer someone up when they are deeply sad. Let go of that. Grief is a natural, healthy process that needs to unfold.

Few things are more grating than trying to be "chipper" in the face of loss. Platitudes in the vein of "Buck up, camper!" or "Tomorrow's a new day!" or "Whatever doesn't kill us just makes us stronger!" are... well, just plain terrible. Likewise, lengthy discourses, letters or cards doling out your wisdom and advice on the situation are equally awful.

If you've earned the place in someone's life to speak truthfully and directly, gently encourage and affirm: "We'll get through this together." "You need to take care of yourself and eat." "Let's take a walk." If you're not sure whether you hold that place or not, you likely do not and should stick to the basics.

2. Don't avoid it.

This seems to be a very popular approach people take to the awkwardness of pain and loss. "Here comes Betty. She's losing her hair from the chemo, poor thing! Well, don't bring it up, just be positive." I can assure you that people experiencing hard realities are thinking about them already. They didn't forget. Bringing it up will not somehow "remind" them of it during a moment when they'd otherwise have forgotten. And avoiding the obvious is often more uncomfortable for them than a sincere and simple inquiry: "Hi, Betty. Good to see you. How are things going with the treatment?"

As noted in the chapter on awkwardness, just acknowledging that you don't know quite what to say is often just the thing: "Hi, Betty. I heard about your news. I'm not quite sure what to say other than I'm so sorry you're going through it."

3. Don't make it everything.

While people experiencing difficult times don't step outside that pain and forget it, it also isn't their entire world— even if it may *feel* at times like it is. So, while avoidance is not best, neither is centering every conversation on the painful situation. If you see the person regularly, there is no need to introduce every conversation with the painful issue at hand. I refer to this as "knowing that we know," which means we've already established open lines of communication about the difficulty going on. If there is any static inside about whether you should say anything, you probably *should*. But if we "know that we know," we can talk about other things.

Many times, people err in the direction of not talking about anything going on their *own* lives, for fear that it may seem selfish or insensitive to mention personal affairs in the face of someone else's loss. In reality, it's often a breath of fresh air for people to just have some normal conversation about the rest of life going on instead of just their own central problem. I find that, once we both "know that we know," simply asking will let you know where to go: "Would you like to talk about it, or would you rather talk about something else for a while?"

4. Don't commiserate.

One of the most tactless things you can do in the face of someone else's loss is to say, "I know exactly how you feel" and then start in, trying to convince the person at length that you *do* somehow know exactly how they feel. Trust me, you don't. Even if you've experienced a similar loss or painful situation, claiming to know how someone feels invalidates *their* experience, because it focuses the attention on you rather than on them and their current pain. And many times, in my observations, sadly enough, it actually *is* an attempt at "stealing the limelight" of attention.

If you hold that place in someone's life as a close friend, and you have experienced similar loss—they know this. A simple "If you want to talk, I'm here" or

"Listen, you *are* going to get through this" intimates that knowledge. And, here again, if you are not sure whether you hold this place—stick to the basics.

It's sometimes tricky when life pain is relayed to us third-person. A friend tells you that his sister just had a miscarriage. Or you ask a neighbor how she is, and she tells you that her son's friend committed suicide yesterday. These people are not experiencing the loss directly, and often this makes it difficult to know what to say. I recommend that you just have some simple and sincere "basics" tucked away for situations such as these, and that you draw on the same few every time to eliminate the awkwardness and guesswork:

"Oh no."

"That's very hard."

"I'm sorry to hear that."

Or simply shaking your head empathetically and saying, "Wow."

I want to touch on a related topic here.

There are some circumstances in a person's life to which we naturally respond as if they are current losses. We share a bus seat with a severely burned teen or see a man with amputated legs at the gym exerting a good deal of effort to get from his chair onto a bench. This causes that awkward sensation, causing us to wonder what to say or how to respond.

Realize that, though these things may feel sad or painful to *us*, if these people are out in public, they are well along the way in their own grief process already and have come to a deeper level of acceptance with their situations. At these times, it is actually *not* best to express sympathy as you would for a loss. This only makes things awkward for the other person. As counterintuitive as it may seem, the advice from my chapter on awkwardness and from this chapter on not avoiding the obvious is best here. People who are handicapped, injured or in some way visibly different— know. If you wind up having an interaction with such a person where you would normally speak to anyone else, introduce yourself and acknowledge the condition with a question or statement of the obvious.

So, I've taken a seat on the bus and realized that a severely burned teen is seated beside me. First, I remember that, while this situation is new to *me* right now, it is not new to the teen. I introduce and acknowledge the obvious:

"Hi, I'm Erik."

"Hi, I'm Chris."

"Hi, Chris. How old are you?"

"Sixteen."

"Do you mind my asking how you were burned?"

This may make some people cringe, to think about asking such a thing. But remember—Chris knows he is burned. It's part of his everyday life. So having someone ask and move on to other conversation is actually refreshingly welcome.

One last note. Don't be confused about my advice on offering "I'm sorry" as a simple condolence. The chapter on apologies does not apply here. This is just one of the many instances where English words and phrases have multiple meanings. Whereas the apologetic "sorry" implies responsibility and remorse, the "sorry" of condolence simply means "I share your sorrow."

Questions for Reflection and Discussion:

APPENDIX page 383

CHAPTER 33

Worry

I WAS TALKING WITH A FRIEND who told me that he had wound up sleeping with an ex-girlfriend. Sparing you the nitty-gritty details, protection measures had malfunctioned, and they wouldn't be sure whether or not she was pregnant for another week or so.

"Do you think I should worry?" he asked, quirking his mouth nervously.

"No," I replied calmly and with a smile.

The tension ebbed from his body with the sigh he exhaled. I am not a doctor, yet it was as if he'd just gotten irrefutable news that she was not pregnant. Curious about his reaction, I asked, "What are you thinking right now?"

"You're smart, and if you think it will be fine, it probably will be," he said.

"I have no idea whether it will be fine or not," I replied. He began to reabsorb any tension he'd expelled moments before. "You asked if I thought you should worry. I don't think you should worry, because it won't change the outcome."

This was not what he wanted to hear. He wanted me to somehow foretell the future and assure him that things would turn out as he hoped. But what I said was the truth nonetheless.

THE BEST ADVICE SO FAR:
Worry serves no purpose but to ruin the present.

Think about that. Try to come up with one positive thing that worry accomplishes.

I'm not talking about care or concern that leads to action. If I get a call that a friend is in the hospital, I will be concerned. And that will lead to action. Concern will move me to stay updated. If I am able, I will drive to the hospital to support family or to see my friend as soon as visitation is allowed. I differentiate this from worry. Worry is a mental obsession that usually leads to inaction.

Everyone worries. We may worry for different reasons, but I've not yet met someone who is so Spock-like that they never worry, simply telling themselves it is "illogical" to do so. Even the most stoic people I know still occasionally worry. But I recommend that worry be redirected as quickly as possible. If not, it has an uncanny way of engulfing and immobilizing us, plunging every otherwise good thing in life into murky shadow.

When I realize that I am worrying about something, I've taken to consistently asking myself a short series of questions about whatever is worrying me:

Is there anything I can do about this *right now*?

If I decide that there *is* something I can do about the problem at that moment — I do it. As simple as this seems, positive action does wonders for alleviating worry.

So, let's say I think someone may be upset with me and I begin to worry about it. I ask myself, "Can I do anything about this right now?" The answer here is likely yes. I can call that person, tell them how I am feeling, and ask them if there's a problem. It's surprising how much time we waste fretting over things that we actually can solve with such a simple action.

If I decide there truly is nothing I can do in the present about whatever is causing my worry, I move to a second screening question:

Is there anything I can do about this at a later time?

Often, this turns up a different result from asking whether there is anything I can do immediately. One of the most common times that worry seizes people is in the middle of the night. And so, in my previous example, I may say to myself, "No, there is nothing I can do right now, because my friend is probably sleeping; but there *is* something I can do tomorrow morning. I can call them then." If I find there is something such as this that I can do at a later time, *I write down what I can do and when.* You may think this seems like a silly step. But I've found that physically writing down that next step does something in the way of symbolically taking the worry out of my head and making it external. There seems to be a component of worry that tells us if we don't keep thinking about something, we'll forget and that this would be catastrophic. To have the worry and its next possible solution written safely down and folded up on the bedside table assures my subconscious mind that I won't forget. And if that niggling worry tries to persist, I just focus my thoughts: "It's OK. I wrote it down.

I will do something about it at that time." Strangely enough, this allows me to sleep in those wee-hours worry spells.

If, however, I've answered that there is nothing I can do at the moment and nothing I can do at any time in the future about what is worrying me—and this is the most important step—I make a deliberate choice to *let it go*. I reiterate to myself that I have done all I can do, and that continuing to worry about this thing any longer is only wrecking good moments in the present. If worrying thoughts come back, I shut them down immediately by reminding myself that I've put the issue to the test and found that it is out of my control.

So I don't try to control it.

Really, isn't that what worry is—a belief that pouring my energy into a situation through worry somehow makes a difference in my ability to control the outcome?

Before closing this topic, let's explore a few more situations and see how they hold up to this short screening process.

It's 2:00 in the morning and I've had a dream that my mother was in a hospital bed, very old and frail, with nearly translucent skin and veins very close to the surface. She is dying. (Yes, I've really had this dream.) I wake up and begin to worry that my mother is getting older and will someday die. I think about how unhappy I will be and how terrible it will be to say goodbye. Now, in reality, my mother is a very healthy and active 68. But worry is hardly logical. So, there I am, my heart pounding and tears stinging my eyes from this dream that seems all too real. Can I do anything about this in the moment? No, I can't. Can I do anything to stop my mother from aging later?

Again, no. Perhaps I'll decide that I will call my mother the next day and tell her that I love her and appreciate her. That's positive. But it won't slow down the clock. So, I'm left telling myself that this falls into the category of something out of my control. I will not allow it to immobilize me or steal good moments I can be having with my mother right now.

My inspection sticker is a week expired and I know I need a new catalytic converter in order to pass. That's going to be about $800, which I don't want to put into a car that already has nearly 250,000 miles on it. But what if I get stopped and get a ticket? Worry sets in, scrambling my thoughts and making me feel trapped in some kind of Catch 22. Can I do anything about it at this moment? Perhaps. If it's a week day, I can decide to drive to the mechanic and just find out what's up. Then at least I'll know what I need to do next. If I'm working, I scribble down "mechanic sticker 4:00" on a scrap of paper, fold it and tuck it in my pocket. There it is. I can't forget it. Or maybe I'll set a reminder to myself on my cell phone. Then, if the worry train comes back, I just pat my pocket or cell phone and refocus. I've got my plan.

Try adopting this simple system for yourself. I'm willing to bet you'll find far fewer moments of a perfectly good present stolen by worry.

Questions for Reflection and Discussion:

APPENDIX page 385

CHAPTER 34

Extremes

AS I PREPARED TO WRITE THIS CHAPTER, an old song from my childhood days was echoing its taunting melody in my mind:

> *Nobody likes me.*
> *Everybody hates me.*
> *I'm gonna go and*
> EAT SOME WORMS!

While my brother and I did once trick a kid into eating gypsy moth caterpillars with the promise that the green innards would turn him into the Incredible Hulk, I'll spare you the more grisly details of that exchange in favor of turning our attentions to the opening lines of this odd little verse. Worms aside, dejected children aren't the only ones to speak in extremes like "nobody likes me" and "everybody hates me" when difficulty presents itself. Think about the number of times you have said or heard comments like these:

"You never listen to me."

"No one appreciates me."

"Nothing in my life is going right."

"I'm the only one who does anything around here."

Such expressions are so commonplace today, in fact, that some might downplay them as simple and acceptable figures of speech. I'd like to suggest however that, on a subconscious level, they are actually quite insidious and destructive.

I once saw a film in which a single mother and her teenage son had a rather rocky relationship. While visiting an estranged aunt, the pair are thrust into some tender moments of real and honest communication. In one particular scene, the mother grabs her son's hand almost fiercely as he is about to walk away from yet another argument. He turns sharply, his eyes threatening. She withdraws her hand quickly and averts her eyes to the kitchen floor. "My feelings for you are like a bowl of fishhooks," she says, now flicking red-rimmed eyes upward to look at him. "I try to pull one out and they all come."

I love this scene and refer to the "bowl of fishhooks" analogy often. Strong negative emotions have a way of causing the details of life to tangle together into one seemingly inextricable mass. It is in these times that we often find ourselves talking in extremes: *always, never, no one.*

THE BEST ADVICE SO FAR:
When negative emotions are strong, discipline yourself to think in specifics rather than extremes.

Extremes serve no purpose other than to allow ourselves to throw a sort of mental tantrum or to wallow in self pity for a while. Extremes are overwhelming. Extremes perpetuate a feeling of hopelessness. If "nothing is going right" for instance, we can justify staying right where we are, without taking action to improve our circumstances. And that is counterproductive.

I've found that it doesn't take much to help someone see that their extremes are unfounded, and that the problem is not as dire as they may have been feeling. Here is a snapshot from a dialog:

Teen: "Everyone's mad at me. I don't have any real friends left."

Me: "I'm not mad at you."

Teen: "I don't mean ... you."

Me: "You said 'everyone' is mad at you. But I am not mad at you. Is your grandmother mad at you?"

Teen: [laughs despite himself] "No, my grandmother is not mad."

Me: "How about Mark and Todd. Are they mad at you?"

Teen: "No, I guess not. No, they're not mad at me. Well, I don't mean *literally* everyone."

Me: "So *everyone* isn't mad at you then. But you clearly feel hurt that *someone* is mad at you. So, tell me who *is* mad at you?"

Frequently, at this point, the actual answer is that one person may (or may not) be mad at the teen. Much of it is perception. But now that the specific problem is identified, a solution can be formulated.

This is nearly always the case with extremes. You'll find that, if you deny yourself the indulgence of using extremes, "No one appreciates me" becomes "I feel hurt that my husband ate out with a friend after I told him I was making dinner."

In the "bowl of fishhooks" analogy, I refer to this process of exchanging extremes for specifics as "pulling one fishhook out of the bowl." No matter how many hooks are tangled in a bowl, we will eventually empty the bowl if we continue to pull out just one at a time.

Questions for Reflection and Discussion:

APPENDIX page 387

CHAPTER 35

Limitations

EARLY ONE AFTERNOON, I was working on some reading skills with a middle-school boy named Dan. He'd come a long way in the short while we'd been working together. And, little by little, I'd watched his confidence build. It' was a wonderful thing to see. Still, he had a ways to go.

One of the most prominent struggles Dan currently had was not with the longer words, but with the simple, everyday ones: *of, to, the, from.* And these can often change the meaning of a sentence. So, I created some timed drills, to help his eyes and brain attune to fine differences in these smaller words. I had typed out 12 short phrases that were quite similar (e.g., *of a word, to the word, to the woods, in the world,* etc.) and explained that he was to do his best to read the list with as few errors as possible, instructing him to key in on vowels and not whole words. He read the list in about forty-five seconds, with 4 errors. I told him he did well, but that I thought he could beat that. I then asked him, "Now, do you think you could read another list of similar phrases without *any* errors, and in under thirty seconds?"

"Nope," he said, matter-of-factly.

And with that, there was no use trying. Because the fact is that we can do virtually nothing that we do not *believe* we can do.

If I don't believe I'm smart, I won't study or learn or show what I know.

If I don't believe I can get a certain job, I will not apply.

If I don't believe my marriage can work, it won't.

It's that simple.

I set the reading exercise aside, instead devoting some time to a pep talk with Dan, reminding him of how far he had come and that he actually *did* have the skills to succeed at this task. I told him that I believed in him, and that I would never ask him to do something that I knew was impossible for him to do. When I saw the light in his eyes begin to shine brighter, I asked him again: "So, do you think you can read the list in under thirty seconds?"

"Yeah," he said, with enough confidence to convince me. That's all I needed to hear. I set the computer in front of him. Not surprisingly, he met the goal with a few seconds to spare.

Any bride or pregnant mom will tell you that you can accomplish much more than you ever thought you could do, if you believe that you can do it, and if you are sufficiently motivated.

THE BEST ADVICE SO FAR:
You can always do more—
and *less*—than you thought
you could do.

OK, you just said to yourself, "Uh… I get the 'more' part. But what's with the '*and less*' bit?"

For many—perhaps most—readers, I could probably have gotten away with the omission of the '*and less.*' But for some of you (like me), those two additional words are 100% necessary. For you, the main problem is not undershooting what you are capable of doing. It's *overshooting*: constantly striving to be better, aim higher, do more. And in and of itself, that is a laudable trait. Sometimes.

I mentioned earlier in the book that I used to have a hard time saying no. In that chapter, I briefly got into my former notion that saying yes was the same as being nice — that I *should* do everything people asked of me, because they wouldn't like me as much if I didn't. But that was only part of the issue.

If I'm being completely honest—to the extent of setting all modesty aside—I also did a lot for people simply because I *could*. And being *able* to do something carried with it a certain assumed expectation that I owed it to the world to do it, or else I was somehow being selfish. The fact is, I can do many things well. Here's hoping that you think me a decent writer, for instance. But in addition to that, I establish rapid rapport with people and find conversation in novel situations both easy and enjoyable. I have played the piano since I was three. In addition, I compose orchestrations, write songs and sing, as well as having some technical skill to record. I am an avid reader with a strong vocabulary. I act. I speak a few languages (though, truth be told, my ultimate dream would be to speak and understand *every* language, not only a few).

I'm an artist and graphic designer. Problem-solving is a solid strength, as is memory and speed of learning, to the point where I actually teach skills in all of these areas to others. And I have creativity to spare.

I know. Aren't I just fantastic?

So, what's with all this horn tooting? I realize that, on paper, it looks like quite the list. Yet being completely honest, I don't *feel* all that unusual. I look at what I do as just—what I do. No big deal. It's the story of my life: there will always be more I want to do than there will be time to do it. I see a dance show on television, and I rue the fact that I didn't take up dance. I see amazing photographs and want to set aside everything else in favor of learning lighting techniques. For every talent or skill I have, I'm still constantly wanting to change "what I want to be when I grow up." It's just the way I'm wired, I guess.

The trouble is that, not only do I want to do everything, I want to do everything *well*. I grew up as a hard-core perfectionist, which didn't help. And so, for most of my life, I was of the mindset that, if I couldn't do something full-tilt, there was no point in doing it at all.

This creates an obvious conundrum. For as much as we may rail against it, we are all human; and that means our personal energy and resources are finite. In short, we are limited.

If ever someone set out to prove this theory wrong, I did. In college, it nearly cost me my life.

I was maintaining a 4.0 GPA, with the mindset that a 3.995 was the same as failure. But I was also more or less a full-time parent to a needy teen boy, as well as spending regular time with a half dozen other kids in similar straits.

And I was also volunteering heavily as a literacy teacher at Job Corps, and giving private ASL lessons on the side. And I was also interning at a psychiatric hospital. And I was also on an international singing team that was planning to travel to Asia in a few months. Add to this keeping up with a social life, doing laundry, running errands and an array of other "betweeners" that make up college life, and you'll understand why both sleep and meals suffered, becoming irregular at best, nonexistent at worst.

One night, I met up with a friend outside her dorm. I started to feel dizzy. She ran inside, and in a few minutes, returned with a large, plastic cup of Tang (oh, the 80s!). As I held it in my hands, it felt strange. It occurred to me as I took the first few gulps that I honestly couldn't remember the last time I'd had a drink. Of anything. I tried hard to remember when the last time I'd eaten was, or what kind of meal it had been. I couldn't.

Moments later, a fire erupted in my gut, spreading out. Fishhooks taking over my body. A few moments later, I was on the ground in a tight ball. *Blackness.* My roommate appeared out of thin air. Then I was somewhere else, over his shoulder, wailing. *Blackness.* I was lying down and couldn't move. Someone jabbed my arm. Red and blue lights. *Blackness.* I'm moving fast. Sirens. I hear my roommate beside me say, "…and then he just collapsed in my arms." I reply, "How romantic." *Blackness.* I'm in a hospital bed. It's the next day. I'm hooked up to a bunch of machines. I still had no idea what had happened to me.

When I was released from the hospital a few days later, my mom called my dorm room. Being a nurse, she asked me many questions about my stats. I learned that she'd been keeping close tabs with the doctors in the ER by phone while I was in the hospital. The best anyone could figure, I hadn't had anything to eat or drink in about ten days.

"But you feel all right now?" she asked, worry in her voice.

"Yes," I said. "I feel fine. Tired and weird that I missed days of my life, but otherwise fine."

Once satisfied that I was, in fact, all right, my mother's quiet concern gave way to the roar of a lioness. "Good! Well, then you're an *idiot*! You nearly killed yourself! Saving the world and keeping up a 4.0 GPA does *no one* any good if *you're DEAD!*" She went on to explain that I'd been in critical condition due to severe dehydration. My temperature had dropped to death's door and, as I recall, certain organs were already beginning to shut down by the time I'd arrived at the hospital.

I've quoted my mother's words many times to myself and others since then: *"You're doing no one any good if you're dead."*

It's true. Aiming high, striving for more, is no longer admirable if it's at the cost of your physical, mental or emotional wellbeing.

It was after this incident in college that the hard reality set in. If I were no longer around, *life would go on*. People would be sad, for certain. But all the things I'd been telling myself *needed* to get done—that needed *me* to do them if they were going to get done right—would still get done without me.

Or they wouldn't. Either way, the world would keep

right on turning just the same. This is a humbling thought. But a realistic one. A healthy one.

I also began to understand and embrace the truth that rest does not equal laziness. And as such, it should not be accompanied by guilt. This brings us back around to the idea of cultivating stillness into our lives. Rather than looking at down time as failing to live up to my potential, I now see regular rest and relaxation breaks as *essential* to reaching that potential. Reaching, I say, and not constantly trying to *exceed* my potential—which is, oddly enough, a complete oxymoron and, moreover, an impossibility.

Further, it is simply not necessary (nor should it be expected) that you do all that of which you are *capable* at all times. It is perfectly reasonable, allowable and healthy to see a thing, to know that you *can* do it, and yet to decline doing it—even if purely for the sake of personal renewal.

Taking care of yourself and knowing your limits is a vital part of helping others as well as yourself. If you are not taking care of yourself, you are in no position to take care of anyone else.

So, yes—live fully, absolutely. Don't sell yourself short. Keep learning and growing. Work hard. Go big or go home.

As long as you *do* sometimes choose to go home.

Questions for Reflection and Discussion:

APPENDIX page 389

CHAPTER 36

Past vs. Present

IN A PREVIOUS CHAPTER, I told you that my mom and I had taken a trip from Boston to North Carolina to see my brother Jason. That was two weeks ago as I'm writing this chapter. By way of quick summary, this visit involved driving down and flying back. The trip there, which would already have been long at 16 hours, turned into 27+ hours when the transmission overdrive on my mom's car kicked out just over the bridge into the Bronx. This required that we drive all the way back home at low speed in the breakdown lane and with the blinkers on, then switch vehicles once back home where we had started—and head right out again that night. Mind you, this was all on no sleep.

Well, this past weekend was the reverse version of the trip. The plan was to fly back down to North Carolina to arrive Friday evening, and then set back out early Saturday morning by car for the return trip home with my mom. You can imagine how this *second* trip—a mere two weeks later—might have seemed to me as I started into it!

I arrived at the airport more than two hours prior to my 3:00 flight. I only had carry-on luggage and had already printed my boarding pass from home, so there was no need to stand in a line at the ticket counter. I went straight to security where, other than my laptop being randomly selected for "testing" with some sort of feather duster, it was uneventful. I was through in less than five minutes. So I bought myself a bottle of water with essence of pomegranate and tangerine, because it seemed like the type of thing people might drink when things were going swimmingly. Then I settled into a chair to read and await boarding.

While waiting (and as had happened many times during the previous two weeks), thoughts about the return drive crept in. I feel I made positive choices in handling that fated erstwhile trip from weeks earlier. But it was still by no means something I was eager to repeat. So, when my mind turned to consideration of the next day's road travel, I reassured myself with certain things.

I told myself that it would be another adventure.

I told myself that I was exceptionally resilient and youthful.

I told myself that I was really proving my mettle.

I told myself how much cooler my party story would seem, after tacking on another 18 or 20 hours of travel within such a short span of time.

I'm not sure I quite believed myself.

It was the best I could do.

Somewhere in the midst of telling myself such things, I became aware that it was approaching 2:15 and there was no plane at the gate. My ticket said boarding would begin at 2:30. When 2:30 and then 2:45 rolled around, still without a plane, people began to stir. The LCD display behind the service counter hadn't changed. It still said 3:00. No announcement had been made as to the nature of the delay or the ramifications to our flight.

Or if there would be a flight *at all*.

I texted my mother and brother in North Carolina to inform them of the delay and to see if they could dig up any more information on their end. No word. I was in the dark.

Around ten-of-three, a plane taxied onto the tarmac nearby. Still no announcements were made to inform passengers. Eventually, the plane circled around and the accordion walkway protruded to meet it. Passengers exited. Food trucks and luggage trains and cleaning crews swarmed around outside. Finally, boarding began. Even if all went smoothly in the air, we would be 30 minutes delayed in landing.

All did not go smoothly in the air.

Approaching Charlotte, the captain's voice came over the speakers, announcing that no planes were being allowed to land, due to thunderstorms over the airfield. We would have to enter a holding pattern indefinitely. If the airport did not give clearance within 20 minutes, we would have to reroute to another airport.

I started mentally running the numbers. Even if things had gone perfectly, I would only have gotten 12 hours at my brother's place before facing the demanding drive the next morning. That number was rapidly dwindling. And now, there was even talk of rerouting to another airport. Just like the last trip, things were starting off on the wrong foot. Or wing, I guess.

Stop.

Consider my last line in the paragraph above. I said,

"*Just like the last trip…*" It's technically *true*. The last trip had presented some unforeseen problems. The current trip was likewise presenting some unforeseen problems. Therefore, it seems perfectly legitimate to say that *this* trip was, in fact, "just like the last trip." Right?

Except that this trip *wasn't* the last trip. This was a *new* trip, with its own set of unique circumstances.

THE BEST ADVICE SO FAR:
Don't color the present with the past.

By allowing ourselves to think that something in the present is "just like" some past thing, we add the baggage of that past thing to our present. We rob ourselves of experiencing the present for its uniqueness and wonder.

Don't we give in to this all the time?

The food or service at a local restaurant isn't quite to our liking on some visit, so we decide then and there that we will never return, launching into a missive about their ills every time we drive by the place thereafter.

A previous employer took advantage of us. So we start updating our résumé as soon as our new boss asks if we might take on some task that isn't technically part of our job description.

A friend betrayed us. So we choose not to trust the next person fully. Or any future person. Ever.

A past lover became controlling or cheated on us. So we see the horns growing from our current partner whenever they make the slightest move without consulting us. Or we turn any mention of their lifelong friend—who happens to be fairly attractive—into an emotional upheaval and certain proof that we really should just break up *now*.

But the wonderful truth is that this server is *not* that server. And this boss is *not* that boss.

This *new* friend is not that *other* friend who hurt us.

This lover is not that *abusive* one.

While I waited for boarding in the airport, I used the extra time to observe.

A teen girl picked up where she'd left off in a novel, turning pages with the kind of fervor and wide eyes and slack mouth that come with total engagement.

A father got on the floor and played a card game with his kids.

An older gentleman pulled his concerned wife in closer and kissed her forehead, smiling.

And later, as we traveled in circles over Charlotte, I looked down and thought, *How many people throughout all of time, past or present, have had the opportunity to witness the awe of a lightning storm—from above it?* Yet there I was, one of them.

We did not reroute. We landed twenty minutes later. My brother was waiting. I got hugs from my niece and nephew upon arrival back at my brother's place. We enjoyed a "comfort meal" of pork loin and potatoes and pineapple casserole, compliments of mom.

And you know what? While there was no way around the fact that the car trip back was still sixteen hours long, it was smooth sailing, without traffic, construction or other incident. The dog slept peacefully in the back seat. Mom and I listened and sang along to music, from her era and mine. We enjoyed the continuation of an audio book we'd started on the trip down. There were many opportunities for good conversation. We learned more about one another.

We let it be *its own* trip instead of the last trip. And it was a good one.

Every journey in life is its own journey.

Today is not yesterday.

In fact, this moment is not the *last* moment. It's *this* one. It's new. It's special.

Let it be.

Questions for Reflection and Discussion:

APPENDIX page 391

CHAPTER 37

Silence

I WAS AT A WINE TASTING in preparation for the wedding of my friends Matt and Kerri. This is funny if you know me. I was in the groom's party, so it made sense for me to be there, I suppose. But I am certainly no aficionado when it comes to wines. I really wish I were. I love the *idea* of knowing your wines and choosing just the right one to go with the braised short ribs. Furthermore, people who hold a wine glass well at a cocktail party just look cool. The inescapable reality for me, however, is that it all tends to remind me of the boxed Easter egg dye kits I used as a kid. But I digress.

One moment, I was standing there trying to remember if the current sample in my glass was a Shiraz or a Malbec, and the next, my friends Holly and Dib were whispering to me furiously in a corner, insisting that I come to Paris with them for a week the following month. Their treat.

The next weeks were a whirlwind. My passport needed to be renewed. I dropped what for me seemed an obscene amount of money on three pairs of Paris-worthy shoes and some belts, piecing together the rest of a suitable wardrobe from a trendy friend's closet. I borrowed a large suitcase (so large, in fact, that I over packed and wound up paying an additional $100 at the airport check-in). And I crammed my head full of French during all spare moments and driving time via audio lessons. This was the trip of a lifetime, and I was determined to live it to the fullest.

Our flight left at four o'clock in the afternoon and, accounting for the time change, had us arriving sometime past six the following morning. After retrieving our bags, a taxi brought us to the street where we would be staying. Unable to check in quite yet, we sat bleary-eyed at quaint round tables outside a little café, eating our first croissants of Paris and drinking cappuccinos. I remember breathing differently, more deeply, as if I were trying to infuse myself with the surroundings, with the realization that I was actually here in Paris. The city was just stirring from sleep. It was quiet. More than once, my friends and I exchanged silent smiles that resulted in welling up—sheer joy at the moment we were sharing. It was too electric to be considered serene. Yet we were too weary for it to have been excitement. It felt like Christmas Eve and contentment.

Afterward, we walked the Seine, taking in the beauty of every lamp post and bridge, waiting for check-in time. Then, we collected our luggage from the travel agency, pulling it along behind us in single file as we made our way to the sixth-floor unit where we would be staying. Once inside, we were all drawn to the first set of windows to our left. Rising up over the lower rooftops, the Eiffel Tower was so close that we had to tilt our heads upward to see its height. Astonishing.

I'm tempted to reminisce about every detail, but I'll

resist the urge and save it all for another book, since I do have somewhere I am alleging to go with my thoughts here. At the end of that first full day, I lay silently in my bed, looking out through the French doors that led to the balcony. The doors were open and a cool breeze flirted with the clean linen draperies on either side. The Eiffel Tower cast its orange glow into the night. I felt like I was trying to take a breath bigger than my body could accommodate. I imagined the others, friends whom I love and who love me dearly, lying in their own beds and having similar thoughts and feelings. My eyes got a sudden sting. If there ever were such a thing as the perfect moment, this was it.

Time slowed in Paris. Life was taken in moments, our thoughts never extending too far beyond the Croque Madame we were enjoying for lunch or playing "Magic Finger": pointing out the items of clothing we wish would magically appear in our closets.

Then one morning, we decided to trek to Notre Dame. Just walking across the cobblestone courtyard to the mammoth cathedral, I was already overwhelmed. It was as if each step were taking me further back in time until finally, reaching the steps, I was transported the full eight centuries to its beginning.

I have never experienced anything close to what I felt as I entered. It was as intense as grief, but without sadness. It was profound. I don't think I breathed for a full minute. But it was not the massive structure alone that overpowered me. It was the hush over the place. Even with thousands of people inside, it was quiet. Soft chanting reverberated among the columns and archways. Here and there, whispered voices rose. Metal tinked as people lit and placed candles. It was not devoid of sound. But it was *quiet*. It was as if everyone were keeping the same secret, agreeing without words to protect it.

Colored light from countless stained glass windows overhead sprawled across grand and dusty paintings, shifting continuously and ever so gradually, while shadows clung to other mysterious recesses. In one large alcove, men and women from around the world reverently awaited confession. In the main sanctuary, others sat in private reflection, interspersed among the rows upon rows of wooden chairs. I could not speak. But I had no desire to, as if speaking would break the spell of wonder that was in place. How many people across the ages have walked across these stones under my feet? Devout people. Murderers. The hopeless and the thankful. I took a seat and closed my eyes. This was not some experience brought on by any particular religious devotion or ideology. It went deeper than that. It was as if the quietude itself were a living thing.

I honestly don't know how long I stayed lost in that state. I would have been content to stay there all day and into the night. But at some point, Dib gently nudged me. I turned to see her smiling with raised eyebrows. She mouthed wordlessly to me, *Ready?* As we exited back into the brightness of the day, an unshaven old man in ragged clothing stood in the courtyard with outstretched arms. His head was tilted back, eyes closed and smiling blissfully, as if he were feeling the sun on his face for the first time. Small birds perched along his sleeves and cap as if he were simply another tree. I had never seen such a sight in my life. Yet, having just left the serenity of Notre Dame, it did not strike me as particularly shocking. It made utter sense somehow.

OK, OK. While this really *is* what happened, and *does* reflect the way I felt, let's close the romance novel for a bit and talk about real life, shall we? Where is the practical advice in all of this?

THE BEST ADVICE SO FAR:
Cultivate silence in your life.

You don't need to travel to far-off lands to benefit from this advice and practice. In fact, my enjoyment of the silent times in Paris was due in large part to my having learned to cultivate silence long before I took that trans-Atlantic flight.

I spoke at Penn State a couple of years ago, as a guest of my friend Chad. As I walked about the expansive campus, I passed or was passed by hundreds of students. I was struck by the uncanny ability of so many people to make so little noise—more like ghosts than living, breathing humans. Some pairs talked quietly between themselves, but the majority looked down, following their feet to wherever it was they were going next. Buses crowded to capacity were likewise oddly quiet.

And yet it *wasn't* quiet.

I would venture to guess that more than 90% of these students donned earphones. Behind curtains of hair, under raised hoods, or simply staring straight ahead—they were shutting out the world around them with barriers of blaring, personalized noise.

But isn't this how most of us are? The small counter

television pumps infomercials into the kitchen as we make our morning coffee. Morning joggers pound the pavement to techno beats. And standard driving procedure now includes deftly pressing buttons to switch between stations in an attempt to avoid as much commercial interruption between our favorite tunes as possible, while children watch DVDs from the back seat. I even know many people who cannot fall asleep without music playing or a television.

On the whole, we've become more and more uncomfortable with silence. Most of us certainly don't enjoy silence when it presents itself, much less would we actually seek it out. But why? What is so terrifying about silence?

Consider that stretch of time late at night, while you are lying in bed, but before you've fallen asleep. (Assume for our purposes that you are not wearing your headphones to bed.) If you're like most people, this small crack of silence quickly begins to flood, like a hole dug near the shoreline. Memories. Worries. Conversations from the day. And we wonder—about everything from how the weather station can be wrong so often, to how we could have managed to stay at our present job so long.

It's not always heavy thoughts, though, is it? Random cartoon images bound through our minds, making us chuckle under the covers. We remember someone we haven't talked to in a while, and wonder how they are doing. Some of us create, thinking of the next idea for our book, or deciding if we will turn the light on and scribble down the song lyrics that just hit us.

Silence is powerful. It's also to a large extent

unpredictable. And it's precisely that unpredictable power which I suspect we find so frightening.

"Cultivate" is one of those words that doesn't get dusted off much anymore. Yet I can't think of a better one to pair with this advice, because it carries many meanings, all of which apply here:

To set aside and prepare for use, so that something can grow.

To improve by labor, care or study.

To further or encourage.

To welcome or become friends with.

Let's look at each of these facets involved in the concept of cultivation, and see how it might apply to silence.

Silence leaves room for thought. Consideration. Reconsideration. In short, silence is one of the major catalysts for change and growth in our lives. Really let that sink in. If we are continually drowning out our own thoughts with noise, yes, it is "comfortable"—but comfort leaves us in exactly the same place tomorrow as we were today. When a farmer cultivates land, he sets it aside and prepares it, knowing that, while it may be hard work, it will pay off with the growth of new crops. So it is with silence. If you are long out of practice in setting aside times of quiet in your life, the first thoughts to rise to the surface may well be painful or uncomfortable. But you're daring enough to try anyway. And in so doing, once the volume is turned down, you realize that your marriage isn't what it used to be. Or that you've become a bit arrogant lately. Or that you've been angry at someone for a long time and not dealt with it. Or that you've wronged someone. *Acknowledging* the truth is the first step to actually *changing* things. We cannot change what we are unwilling to acknowledge.

For some, the "toil" of silence may be that your mind feels empty. Blank. And that feels uncomfortable. I would suggest that this feeling of the void of silence is false. While there are occasional times that we are so overworked or overwhelmed that we truly "zone out," most often the perception that we have no thoughts is actually a cover-up of sorts. The mind so dreads the thoughts that come up that we snip them off even as they emerge from the soil of silence. It's so much a part of our defense, in fact, that we become unaware that we are doing it. If this sounds like you, try being silent around a central question. *How are my relationships lately? Who do I consider my close friends and why? What do I like about myself?* It doesn't really matter what you choose as a question. A focusing question like this pondered in silence is virtually guaranteed to foster self-awareness and solid thought.

That said, let's suppose that you actually do continue to work the soil of silence and begin to take steps to address the issues that turn up. You make decisions to correct less flattering character traits. You have conversations that have been a long time in the coming. Relationships improve. Before long, you find that an immense amount of internal static dies down. There is less *need* to drown it out with external noise. Like tilling rocky soil, it's hard

work to address the thoughts that silence brings us—
and the actions they might require on our part. But
the payoff is enormous and life changing.

The second definition of "cultivate" speaks of
improvement, through labor, care or study. You see, though
cultivating silence may at first seem like labor, the silence
begins to be filled not with difficult realizations, but with
an entirely new sort of thoughts. As the silence becomes
less of a chore, room is opened to learn more about yourself
and others—about the world going on around you. Greater
care is taken in noticing the simple things that were
being obscured by busyness and noise. In fact, you will
find that even focus and memory improve as the mind
has unbroken periods of quietness in which to process
information and make new connections. You may find
creativity that you had thought was lost to childhood.
In short, things improve. Quality of life—of living—
improves.

Now beginning to experience the newfound benefits
of silence, you start to actually enjoy times of silence.
You look forward to them. You look for ways to expand
them, to "further and encourage" the things that happen
when distractions are minimized. Perhaps you learn
to journal your thoughts so that you can continue
developing them the next time.

And then, little by little, you find that you are
no longer afraid of silence. It becomes your friend and not
your enemy. You finally get what was meant by the saying
"Silence is golden." You stop running from yourself
and your thoughts. You instead become someone who
listens to your thoughts, welcomes them, trusts them,

changes and grows regularly, and knows the benefits this brings. And you've found something that, for the majority of people, remains always out of reach: peace.

Cultivating silence isn't about adding "another thing" to your busy life—to spend hours doing yoga or meditating by candlelight (though, if you get to the point of loving silence, go for it!). It's mostly about choosing to restructure events that already exist in your day. Try driving one leg of your commute without listening to the radio or using your cell. Decide to walk to certain classes or do your Monday morning jog without headphones. Turn off the TV during meals at home. And remember—the goal is not silence for the sake of silence. It's not a punishment. It's a choice, one made with the goal of seeing personal change and growth.

I know there are those who will read this and think, "But you don't know my life. There is no time to be quiet." The young mother with the hyperactive two-year-old who never naps comes to mind. Still, while I truly do sympathize, making time for silence is perhaps even more important for you. Without it, life can quickly turn into being more machine than person, losing yourself and your relationships in the process. Be creative. If you can't get a babysitter for a few hours a week, consider trading off with a friend, where you take their child for a while one day, and they take yours another. Don't give in to the idea that you have no say in the matter. You do.

Finally, please understand. I am a musician and music lover. I love conversation. And I have my shows that I enjoy watching. I'm not advocating some austere lifestyle that would have you rivaling the convents and monasteries of the world (though several friends of mine find these places to be wonderful retreats when they need to create space to be silent). I'm simply encouraging you to become comfortable with silence and to build it into your life on a regular basis. Even the music in your headphones will begin to sound different.

Questions for Reflection and Discussion:

APPENDIX page 393

CHAPTER 38

Boredom

ILOVE THE OCEAN. I especially love it in the middle of the night, when the beach is empty and the sky is full. There is something about hearing the sound of the surf pulling the smooth, tumbling stones and shells over one another that sifts the gunk out of the soul. Some of my most treasured memories are of sitting in the sand with close friends beside me, looking out there, listening. Talks go deep in those times, but silence is never uncomfortable. The ocean reminds me of the bigness of things, of possibility and of how connected we all really are.

When I was small, I used to imagine that the ocean was alive, and that it liked me best. I still feel that way sometimes.

I'm by no means one to avoid the ocean during the day, however. I have often said that, for me, the word "vacation" can easily be summed up in one image. Beach chair. Toes digging into the wet sand at the surf line. Sun on my face. Cool water lapping at my feet. A friend beside me. And a good book. I guess I'm easy.

Often, when I'm at the beach during busy hours, I hear children complaining that they are bored. "There's nothing to do," they whine, as baking parents murmur suggestions from prone positions. It still amazes me that anyone could be bored at the ocean, let alone a child. It makes me wonder if all our technology has truly robbed us of our imaginations.

When I was growing up, I spent a good deal of time on the beach every summer. We'd cross the Bourne or Sagamore Bridge into Cape Cod. Driving further in, the trees would begin to change from maple and elm to stouter scrub pine and juniper, and the salt in the air would thicken. Whichever home we'd rented for that summer would seem perfect, like we'd gotten the very best one on the street. But most of our days were spent on the beach.

There was a little inlet at our usual beach where, during high tide, I could throw my minnow trap. I'd place some broken mussels or razor clams inside, latch it closed, and plunk it in, pinning the frayed rope to the sand with a rock or staking it in place with a piece of driftwood. You'd always catch something. Sometimes, it would just be small shiners. Sometimes larger minnows. If you were really lucky, you'd catch a small eel. Whatever you caught, you'd transfer it to a plastic bucket and try to make its temporary home as comfortable as possible by adding sand and rocks and seaweed. To this might be added some hermit crabs, snatched from the sandy bottom while snorkeling. If you were really cool, you'd just dive under without a mask and open your eyes, letting the sea salt burn them, and prove your worth by coming up with something that was alive. The makeshift zoo-in-a-pail would elicit the usual caution when presented to my mother: "Don't keep them too long. All of the oxygen will be out of the water soon."

Sometimes, the goal was not to catch, but to observe. To learn. I could spend whole days with my mask on, walking slowly through tide pools with my face in the water and my tail end in the air. I loved to have my ears underwater during these excursions. It was as if the real world had disappeared and I was an accepted citizen of the world below the surface, a mer-boy. My back and neck would bake, but I didn't mind. It was a small price to pay for the wonders I was fortunate enough to behold.

When it got too late to see underwater, you'd dig a hole. There was a feeling of personal pride when you'd get below sea level and start to see the water seep in. The further back from the water's edge you were when achieving this, the cooler you were. Even more noteworthy was if you had the tenacity to dig a hole big enough for you to fit in. And if you were *really* daring, you'd have your brother or your cousin bury you in it, up to your neck. Then, after a few minutes of the illusory decapitation, you'd struggle with all your might against the cold, wet sand exerting its force upon you, pinning your arms to your sides. Slowly, mightily, you would rise, feeling the sand give way around you until you emerged victorious, feeling as if you'd really accomplished something.

Even now, at this very moment, if you were to go out to my car and open the trunk, you would see a minnow trap. I figure you just never know when you might need one.

I was mid-May as I was writing this chapter. Beach days were coming. But I didn't have to wait for them in order to have an adventure.

Just the night before, I had gone into Boston to hang out with a new friend, Mark. He lived in an area of the city I'd never been to, so that in itself was an adventure. We walked a few blocks deciding what to eat for dinner. At one corner, my friend stopped and pointed to a building ahead. "Do you like sushi?"

"Sure, why not! I haven't had much of it," I admitted, "but I liked what I had. I'm up for anything."

Inside, we perused the menu. He seemed like he might know more about sushi than I. "Why don't you just pick and I'll enjoy whatever you get," I offered. He scanned the menu with a furrowed brow, which left me wondering if he were concentrating or feeling overwhelmed with having been give the reins on the decision.

"We're still getting to know one another," I interjected. "So tell me, are you the type who feels confident about being asked to choose for both of us ... or does it make you feel stuck?"

"Stuck," he smiled, obviously relieved that I'd asked.

"Let me take care of it, then," I said smiling back. Is there anything you *don't* like?"

"Tuna," Mark replied.

"OK, well, I hope you're up for a mystery dinner then!"

When a young woman came to take our order, I said, "Hi! My friend and I are in the mood for an adventure tonight, and I wonder if you would help us. Would you just bring us a mixed plate of anything you think is delicious— anything except for tuna—and we will love whatever you choose for us."

She smiled with a raised eyebrow. "Anything?"

"Yes, anything," I said. "I know that whatever you pick will be the perfect thing."

She nodded graciously and headed for the kitchen.

"I'll have to remember to do that in the future!" my friend said. "I never would have thought to!"

I told my friend about another notable time I'd done this. The previous year, for my birthday, my friend Chad and I used an app on his phone to find a restaurant. We entered the details:

Type: African

Price: mid-range

Distance: within 50 miles

We found ourselves at a tiny, authentic Nigerian restaurant a state away. Much as I'd done at the sushi restaurant, we told our very warm and engaging server, "You know what? We are in the mood for an adventure! Surprise us. Bring us any two separate dishes that you yourself would eat and find amazing." Forty minutes later, he returned, meals in hand.

"These are two very delicious dishes," he explained with great pride, in his thick Nigerian accent. "I would have this one every day for a mid-day meal, and this one for dinner. They are both very nice." He gestured toward each of the items on our plates. Some bitter vegetables flavored with bone shards, of which we were cautioned to be mindful while eating it. A gelatinized ox hoof. Some fish over spiced rice. Yucca root paste. And tripe. I cannot explain to you how my friend and I described the taste of tripe to one another that night if I want to keep this book family friendly, but suffice it to say that it lies somewhere in the realm of rubber bands and dog doo.

But I loved that night. That meal. The laughs we had. Our waiter and his stories. Because it was a new experience. I felt present and alive.

THE BEST ADVICE SO FAR:
Do something new every day.

I can honestly say that I have never in my life been bored on my own time. Sure, I've been less than interested while sitting through mandatory policy meetings at jobs, or wading through the long-form Latin mass at a wedding. But any time when I am free to do as I please, I cannot imagine being bored. That does not mean I am always *wild,* or even that I am *busy*. Rest and relaxation are not boredom. I'm talking about that feeling that "there's nothing to do." It's foreign to me.

When my siblings and I were teens, one of us would occasionally complain aloud that there was "nothing to eat." And my mother would reply, "Well, there's nothing that's going to jump out of the cabinets or refrigerator onto your plate, if that's what you mean. But there's plenty to eat."

I think we often expect life to jump out of the cabinets onto our plate, and we feel cheated when it doesn't. Or, worse yet, we don't expect anything. Just the repetition of the same circular path we walked yesterday.

News flash: it's a big world out there!

Doing something new doesn't have to mean taking a trip to Tahiti or leaping from a plane. It doesn't even have to cost one red cent.

I met up with my friend John for dinner after his shift

at the hospital one night. We met at a local chain restaurant that was midway between our homes. It was late. He was still in his scrubs.

On his birthday, which had been just a few days prior, I had texted him: "Happy Birthday! Do something new today—something you've never done before! Report back." He hadn't reported back. So I asked him as we waited for our meals whether or not he had taken me up on my challenge. He admitted that he had not. "I thought about it," he said with a sheepish smile, "but I really just couldn't think of anything."

"What about eating something you'd never tried before?"

He shook his head, "I tried to think of that. Nothing came to mind."

"Well, have you ever lain down on a sidewalk in public?"

John blurted out a laugh, flooding his weary face with a bit of color. "No. No, I can't say that I have." It took him a couple of seconds to realize that I wasn't kidding.

"Well, then that is what we're going to do," I informed him. "When we leave here, we are going to lie down on the sidewalk and just look up at the stars for a minute."

"I don't think so," he countered with a challenging grin.

Our meals came and we continued to chat about living a life that matters. About not living in predictable patterns. About doing new things that lead to new ideas, new perspectives, new possibilities. After paying the bill, we headed outside.

"Come on," I goaded, eyeing the sidewalk just outside

the door. "It won't kill you. Can't hurt. Might help!" I lowered myself to the ground, hoping he would follow suit.

To my surprise, he did.

We lay there, looking up at the stars overhead for a minute or so. Some late guests got out of their nearby car and had to actually walk around us to enter the restaurant. They giggled. My friend didn't move.

I was actually the one to break the silence, finally stirring to get up. He did the same.

"So…" I prodded "…how do you feel?"

"Stupid," he said. We laughed. "It *certainly* was a new experience, though. Thanks." And then we went our separate ways for the evening.

Not long after, this friend began reading a book I'd given him for Christmas. I'd asked him many times since January if he'd started it yet, and his reply had always been the same: "not yet." It was now August, and he was finally reading it. Within a week of the seemingly trivial (and admittedly odd) act of lying on a sidewalk, he'd picked up the book—which happened to be about breaking out of cycles and pushing yourself to live fully.

I truly believe that it doesn't matter *what* new thing you do every day, as long as you do something. Stop and look around a shop that's along your usual route, yet that you've never visited. A watchmaker or a pet store. Take a different route to work one day, even if it's a little out of the way and you have to argue with your GPS over it. Take a walk down a side street you've never been down. Find a new vocabulary word and use it with a few people that day. Read a book in a new genre. Learn to tie a full

Windsor knot. Go to a department store and try something on that you wouldn't normally see yourself wearing.

I'm convinced that most boredom is just laziness in disguise. As you make it a challenge to do something new each day, you'll find that what started out as racking your brain will become easier and easier. You may even wind up starting a bucket list. Creativity will expand. You'll feel more awake and alert. Fresh ideas will occur to you at work. Conversations will become more interesting. There's a certain cumulative energy to it all. And at the risk of repeating myself too often, doing something new is a reminder that you always have a choice.

So what are you waiting for? Put the book down for a bit and go do something new!

Questions for Reflection and Discussion:

APPENDIX page 395

CHAPTER 39

Lemonade

WHEN I SEE A KID running a lemonade stand, I get excited. I remember the thrill of *being* that kid. Coloring the sign to announce your wares, sure that your graphic artistry and marketing were going to practically pull the people in, almost against their will. Hearing the satisfying "pah!" as you peeled back the plastic lid on the tub of powdered drink mix and were greeted with *that* smell. Choosing a pitcher that would make the lemonade look most appealing (always glass for me; never plastic). Cracking the ice from the trays into the finished product (having forgotten to do this first, and thus making quite a mess with the splashing). And sometimes, mom would suggest adding lemon wheels she'd cut for you, in order to make it look more authentic and to up the ante.

The card table and folding chairs would be set up close to the road. The sign was affixed with masking tape:

ICE COLD LEMONADE
10¢

It was imperative that the sign say "ICE COLD," because that was part of the sure-fire marketing strategy. The pitcher of lemonade was placed front and center, with two upside-down stacks of plastic cups waiting beside.

The tin can would occupy the corner of the table closest to yourself, so that you could look into it often. The *money* can. I remember the feeling of anticipation in setting it all up while watching the cars go by on the nearby road. Every one that passed before we were open for business was a missed opportunity to start filling that can.

And you imagined that can *full*. The night before, and that morning as you prepared, you'd do and re-do the figures. "If *this* many cars stop, then I'll make *this* much, and if *THIS* many cars stop, I could make *THIS* much," and so on. Then, of course, you'd begin to break it all down by the hour.

You felt confident. Important. Grown up somehow.

Show time! *OK, world, let's see those dimes!* But then…

Much to your confusion, the cars would *not* stop. There would *not* be a waiting line that was impossible to keep up with. The can would *not* be getting full. And then your aunt would stop by. Or your grandmother. Or a neighbor. And your mom would suggest that you make the sign bigger with darker letters. Or that maybe if you smiled and waved and didn't look quite so dejected, that might do the trick.

You'd inevitably give in and drink some of the profits away as the afternoon wore on. *How are all these people not as hot as I am? How are they able to resist my lemonade?* you'd think, never quite aware that the ice had all melted by now, and that the lemonade was diluted and warm.

But then—once in a while—someone would stop. A stranger. A *real live* customer. And you'd get your game face on, and sit up a little straighter, and say "Hello!" instead of "Hi." And you'd pour him a brimming, shaking cup of your warm, iceless lemonade. And instead of a dime, he'd produce a whole *dollar!* And you'd thank him and offer him more lemonade, which he'd refuse and tell you that you'd need it for other customers, and that he was sure this was the time of day when most people really got the hankering for lemonade. And you'd wave after him as he drove away. Then you'd grin at your dollar, wide eyed. And you'd refill that pitcher and add some more ice and wipe your brow. By gum, you were back in it!

THE BEST ADVICE SO FAR:
Never pass a lemonade stand without stopping.

I've made it my goal to be *that guy.* The guy who always stops, whether he is thirsty or not. The guy who saves the day. Who gives the whole dollar (and sometimes a five) with a wink and tells them how terribly thirsty he was, and that he really didn't know what he would have done had they not had that lemonade stand.

The ability to take someone else's perspective goes beyond literature and lemonade stands. It's a conscious choice to really *see* the others around us. To value them. To empathize. And to engage.

A me-centered life is a lonely and strangely unsatisfying one. Self is never satisfied. The more we feed it, the hungrier it gets.

On the other hand, choosing to adopt more others-centered attitudes and actions connects us, bringing with it a sense of joy, belonging and purpose.

It's Memorial Day weekend. Summer is here. Be on the lookout for the lemonade stands near you.

And stop.

Questions for Reflection and Discussion:

APPENDIX page 397

CHAPTER 40

Laughter

MY NEARLY THRITY-YEAR FRIENDSHIP with Bud and Dib got off to a fast and furious start. The first day I met them, we had lunch. And for the next year or two, I was at their house nearly every night until 2:00 A.M. Often, it was more like 3:30. And, yes, we had jobs.

Bud would usually be the first to fade, which made for great fun as Dib and I put various objects—not all of them edible—into his slack mouth, holding our hands over our own mouths as we silently cracked up. It seemed no matter how late it got, we'd get our fingers out like a first grader doing math and count off how many hours of sleep we could still get if we stayed up just *one more* half hour.

And then, of course, I had the 40-minute drive home. How we managed such hours is a mystery to me, only explicable by the dim notion that we must have been very young once.

One such occasion lives on in particular infamy. On that night, a new phrase was coined, one which has defined many a moment since.

It was well past 3:00 A.M. by that time, and we were exchanging the usual prolonged goodbyes in the kitchen when it happened. My eyes glazed over, and I began to sway, an idiot's vapid grin taking over my face. The last thing I really remember while standing was Dib's eyes widening as her mouth formed words in slow motion. "Oh boy…"

Then I was down. On the floor in a ball. Giggling maniacally. It was really more like screeching, if I'm being completely honest. Whatever it was, it robbed me of breath, of motor control. Of sanity.

Bud and Dib crouched over me with a mixture of concern and fascination, like city folk watching a horse give live birth for the first time. Every word they said to try to elicit a response from me seemed like the funniest joke I'd ever heard. The only response I could manage for the first five or ten minutes was peals of laughter, interrupted only by my body's self-protective measures as it struggled to keep me breathing.

You see, a mental picture had formed in my mind. Well, it sort of took over my mind. It isn't even that funny from where I sit now. But in that moment, for whatever reason, it was all there was in the universe. I was in the throes of it. I drifted through the expanse of it. It had me in its grip. Hard.

Over the course of—and I'm really not exaggerating— the next thirty minutes, I eeked out an explanation in one- or two-word pants, the laughter mounting to shrieks, my face and hair damp with tears. I hurt everywhere, which also seemed somehow indescribably funny to me in that state. Pain! Funny! Yes!

Enter the funhouse of my deranged imagination— if you dare.

In my mind's eye, I was standing at a hall closet door.

I was compelled to open the door, though I knew I probably shouldn't. But I did. Immediately, the weight of whatever lay inside bore against the door, forcing it open toward me. I tried and tried to shut Pandora's Box, but the force mounted against me. After a few more seconds, the closet burst open, and an endless pile of Kermit the Frog dolls flew down on top of me. Each Kermit landed with its own little *squeak* —somewhere between the sound of a bike horn and a dog's chew toy. An interminable, squeaking rain of Kermits was burying me alive.

You can imagine my shock and dismay. Of course, this was all in my mind. But it was hysterical all the same. Really riotous stuff, I tell you.

That is the picture I saw—the mental image that might have ended a less stalwart friendship. Thereafter, that special place in the wee hours, where any and everything becomes side-splittingly amusing, has been dubbed "Kermit's Closet." No sooner do the eyes glass over than Dib will shake her head and say, "Oh boy, watch out. Kermit's Closet is opening."

THE BEST ADVICE SO FAR:
Laugh.

One of my favorite questions to ask people is "When was the last time you laughed so hard that you cried and your stomach hurt?" It's astonishing to know just how many people really can't remember the last time. That's a shame. My last time was this afternoon, joking with Chad while we had "office hours" on the phone.

The time before that was this morning. All by myself.

I'd had a ridiculous dream that I was a German wrestler. The stakes were high. It was all very serious in the dream. But when I woke up, the juxtaposition with reality had me in stitches for a solid minute. Great way to start the day.

They say that laughter is the best medicine. There are countless studies to support the truth of this old adage. And that begs the question, what kind of funk does our soul wind up contracting if we *don't* take our medicine?

Laughter is cathartic. It keeps things in perspective. It prevents us from taking ourselves too seriously. I'm not suggesting that everyone needs to brave Kermit's Closet (though it is a fun visit). But I can personally vouch for the benefits of learning to laugh, and doing so often.

Questions for Reflection and Discussion:

APPENDIX page 399

CHAPTER 41

Being an Adult

I T'S THE FOURTH OF JULY AGAIN as I write this. Today is all things summer. Sunshine. A perfect breeze. The parade down Main Street. An excitement in the air. A sense that some things really matter.

When I was a young boy, summers lasted forever. I was attuned to the smells of worm dirt (you know—dirt that you're sure has worms in it, whether you see them right now or not?) and things that grow in ponds. And rain.

Oh, and the smell of sunburned skin. And Noxema. And no matter how bad it hurt while you slept, you'd say it didn't at all, just because people told you how much it would, and because you wanted to be cool.

Being barefoot was the norm. Hopping out of the car and across stove-hot blacktop, sucking in air between tight teeth, was exquisite—the dare before the payoff of toes digging into soft sand. Even the omnipresent green and red metal trash barrels that are placed at beach entrances, smelling strongly of ketchup and cigarettes, seemed to have a sort of fantastic quality to them. It didn't matter if I'd been there all week, or even several times that day, cresting the dunes and seeing the ocean unfold before me—hearing it roar and shush over thousands of tumbling pebbles — filled me with breathless exhilaration.

It still does.

Back then, schedules consisted of items like these:

1. Wake up without an alarm clock.
2. Eat three bowls of sugar cereal.
3. Watch some cartoons.
4. Go outside and follow a line of ants around.
5. Maybe collect ants in a jar of dirt, for further study.
6. Look for salamanders. Or Indian arrowheads.
7. Read a few chapters in a can't-put-down fantasy novel.
8. Get called for lunch.
9. Have a peanut butter and banana sandwich.
10. Go back outside and jump off stuff.

Last night, I was talking with some friends over a barbeque. Someone exclaimed how much faster time goes by as we get older. This was followed by the typical grunts of grudging agreement, much wagging of heads, and commentary about how "kids just don't know what they're in for."

But is adulthood really meant to be no more than some cautionary tale with which to frighten children? "Don't grow up—or *this will happen to you!*"

I think we're missing something here.

THE BEST ADVICE SO FAR:
Stay childlike.

Some years back, I was hanging out with a group of high school seniors—guys whom I'd mentored since their freshman year. College was on their minds and they'd been very heavy with the weight of "becoming an adult." It bordered on morose.

I asked them to go around and name things that they loved to do before the age of ten. "Don't value judge it. Just put it out there." Here were some of the things they mentioned:

> "Splashing in puddles after it rained."

> "Going 'exploring' in the woods."

> "Making up yard games of Good Guys
>   vs. Bad Guys."

> "Catching fireflies in jars."

We talked like this for almost two hours. The more they reminisced, the lighter the mood got. The room was all smiles and laughter and excited interjections. "Oh, *yeah*! Me, too!"

In the middle of the reverie, approaching 9:30 at night, Chad blurted, "That's it. We're all going to camp out on the beach tonight in tents. And we're going to swim. And we're going to dig an eight-foot hole in the sand. It's already done in my mind." (He says this last bit a lot, and I'd be lying if I said it wasn't mighty catchy.)

No sooner had he finished than the room was swirling with activity as the guys headed for cars, talking over each other on their way to the lot about who had tents and shovels and flashlights (and wondering out loud if they would get arrested).

Two hours later, there we were—on the beach together, playing Frisbee under the light of a full moon, laughing. And by gum, we dug that eight-foot hole. The heaviness of "adulthood" was a phantom. It couldn't touch us.

The fact is, there is no rule that says adults can't do the things we loved to do as kids. Why *don't* we splash barefoot in puddles after a warm rain anymore? Really. Clothes come clean in the wash just as well today as they did back then. Maybe even better, what with all the nifty improvements in detergents.

Why *can't* we go exploring again? Or catch turtles? Or collect fireflies in a jar?

The answer is... *we can.* Not only can we, we really *should.*

I consider myself a fairly well-adjusted, mature and responsible guy. And I still do these things. What's more, I'm happy. I stopped for a while, some years back, because I gave in to the unspoken lie that being childlike was *childish.* Immature. Looked down upon. That adults are very serious creatures, for whom "fun" must not exceed the occasional baby shower or book club. Or watching televised sports.

That is simply not true.

I'm convinced that time goes by faster as we get older because we stop living in the present. We begin to mark time by deadlines. When the next paper has to be turned in. How long I have to get my grades up before marking closes. When the mortgage is due. How many weeks

I have to get money together to buy everyone Christmas gifts. How many years before I can retire.

How many years I might have left before I die.

That is not living. Kids know how to *live*. And that is why childhood summers last forever.

I am not saying "don't plan." I am saying that we can intentionally retain some childlike wonder, risks and spontaneity. We can learn to take ourselves a whole lot less seriously. Staying childlike is key to actually enjoying the responsibility and freedom that comes with being an adult.

So what did *you* love to do as a kid? And what's keeping you from doing it.

Questions for Reflection and Discussion:

APPENDIX page 401

CHAPTER 42

Wonder

I SAT LOOKING OUT THE WINDOW, waiting for one of the kids who would be arriving soon. I noticed a bird perched not more than five feet away. I slipped around the window until I was hidden by the wall, and slowly opened the window so that I could get a better look, without the glare on the glass. Then I returned to the couch to observe. The bird's tail bobbed sharply and rhythmically, up and down, up and down. Every few seconds, it ruffled its feathers all over, then rotated its head around backward, preening. I took note of the markings: brown back, flecked with black and white; black crest and throat; white chest and mask.

In doing this, I had a visceral memory from childhood. We had a large, open yard that was home to many animals. I had come across a bird floundering in the grass. As it saw me approaching, it thrashed, panicking. I remember sending out with all my might my "I'm not going to hurt you" vibe, which I was certain animals could hear (you'll be hard pressed to convince me they can't even now). Slowly, I crouched down and reached out my hands. The bird didn't fight it. Gently, I picked it up, being careful not to force the injured wing into any position. I remember the weight of that bird. Its heat. The sheen of its black eyes, so close. Feeling the rapid flutter of its heartbeat against my palm.

I took the bird inside to my mother, a nurse. I knew that she could fix the wing. My mother acted as though my bringing this creature inside was the most natural of things. She held out her hands and I gingerly transferred the tiny patient to her. She held it up in front of her face and gave it a looking over. "It's a starling," she said. I was fascinated that she knew what kind of bird it was just by looking. "Yup. It's wing is broken."

My mother sent me out to find some small worms. With urgency, I did so and brought them back. By that time, my mother had constructed a makeshift nest out of soft fabric, in which the bird was resting comfortably. My mother mashed the worms with some warm milk and sucked some of the formula up with an eyedropper. She ran the tip of the dropper along the edge of the bird's clamped beak, releasing a drop. I watched wide-eyed, wondering if this would work. The droplet of white ran along the ridge of the beak and disappeared. Then, as if a switch had been turned on, the bird flung its mouth wide open, waiting. My mother placed the eyedropper deep inside and squeezed the plunger. The bird's throat pulsated. This ritual went on a few more times before my mother stopped, despite the bird's protests.

My mother cared for the starling as if it were an infant, feeding it every few hours, even through the nights. The wing had been set, though I can't describe exactly how she'd done it. In a couple of weeks, she announced that it was time to see if the bird's wing was strong enough to fly. We took it outside. It was in no hurry to leave and we had to coax it. This was a bit of a conflict for me. My eyes stung with sadness to say goodbye. I was worried that the bird might feel we no longer wanted it, that this was why we were shooing it along into the yard. I sent out my vibes again, stronger than ever: "It's time to fly! We love you! And you can come back any time!"

The starling hopped forward, looking back. It fumbled with its wing. Had it forgotten how to fly? Hop. Hop. It ruffled its feathers all over. The wings flexed. It turned its head around backward, as if checking the engines. One more hop and then—

Off it went. My heart soared with it. It worked! He surely would have been eaten by a predator had I not found him. And my mother, who was more magician than nurse in my mind, had fixed it.

So, here I was, sitting on my present-day couch, watching this new bird and remembering. The bird began twitting its call: *chip — chip — chip — chip — cheroo.* I remembered the thrill of knowing what a starling *was.* This bird was definitely *not* a starling.

Why is it that we lose our sense of wonder as we leave childhood? Why do tide pools and ants and the veins of leaves—or the curiosity to know *what kind*—lose their ability to fascinate us? I pondered this. One possibility is that, as children, we are encountering so many things for the very first time. Perhaps *newness* was a primary ingredient in wonder. And, in a verb sense of the word "wonder," I suppose that is true. I cannot *wonder* about what I already know.

Yet, in the noun sense, I think wonder—a *sense of wonder*—is something we can keep for a lifetime. I think it is not something we necessarily *lose*, but something we *let go* for the sake of trading it for "more adult things" like… like… jobs. And bills. And being serious. And looking straight down, to be sure my feet take exactly the same steps they took yesterday.

THE BEST ADVICE SO FAR:
Never lose your sense of wonder.

My perched friend flitted off and I grabbed my laptop from the coffee table. I did a quick search: *Massachusetts birds*. This led me to several sites filled with pictures. I was surprised to see the sheer number of birds native to this area! I scanned through the pictures. I narrowed it down to three. From there, I followed links to sites for bird calls, where I listened to recordings. The first was definitely ruled out. The second was a maybe. The third— was it. *Chip — chip — chip — chip — cheroo*! I'd found it! I'd been observing a house sparrow.

And you know what? Just as I had all those years ago when I was a small boy, I was thrilled at knowing. I felt connected to the world in a new way. I now knew what a house sparrow was by sight and by call.

Of course, keeping—or regaining—a sense of wonder goes beyond gaining mere academic knowledge. If you know me at all, you will not be surprised to find that, like so many things, I believe maintaining a sense of wonder at the world around us—is a choice.

A choice to take time for little things.

A choice to admit that we don't know it all.

A choice to take ourselves a little less seriously.

A choice to notice.

And that, of course, affects how we view everything—and *everyone*—along the way.

Questions for Reflection and Discussion:

APPENDIX page 403

CHAPTER 43

Going Beyond

IN A PREVIOUS CHAPTER, I mentioned Brandon, the boy I had taken in for a year-and-a-half when I was just out of college. He was not the only one.

I first met John in a crack house. Lest you think I'm shady, I went into said establishment to retrieve another young man I thought might be in trouble there. John was slouching in a dirty green recliner. Though the room was already dark and filled with smoke, he wore aviator-style sunglasses, partly covered by his long black hair, which hung in front of his face and across his shoulders. The rest of his outfit was composed of a black Guns-N-Roses T-shirt, faded black jeans, and combat boots. A cigarette hung from a corner of his mouth in a way that seemed set on letting everyone know exactly how much he didn't care. I smiled and said, "Hey." He jutted his chin at me, which I took as a form of greeting. That was the whole of our first encounter.

After that, I'd see John hanging out around other kids in parking lots in the town adjoining mine. I always stopped to say hi. Chin jutting turned to "hey" or "'sup," and after a period of gradually lengthening exchanges, we had our first real conversation, sitting on a curb late one night.

John was 15. He had been smoking since he was in grade school, drinking and using since junior high. He lived with his mother, also a user who got her drugs from John, who could buy them for her cheaper at school than she could from her adult sources. He didn't know his father, though he'd heard that he lived somewhere in his home town of Attleboro. John was a poor student. His life's dream was to be an auto mechanic, and so the other courses seemed a waste to him. At the time we talked, he had never been on a plane. He had never been out of state. He had never seen the ocean.

In fact, he had never been out of the city of Attleboro in his life.

My first attempt at broadening John's horizons was to invite him over the town line to my home in Norton. I told him that I had a movie I wanted him to watch. He was sure he wouldn't like it. So I made him a deal. He could "make" me watch any movie he liked, and afterward, he would have to watch my movie without complaint. He raised an eyebrow and formed a devilish grin. "*Any movie I want, huh?*" I confirmed, hoping against hope that it wasn't going to be the worst skin flick he could conjure up.

The night arrived. John and I got pizza. He was being very mysterious about the film to which I would soon be subjected. He said it was one of his favorites. I couldn't begin to guess.

As it turned out, his movie choice was *Harold and Maude*, a dark comedy about a depressed teenage boy who falls in love with a 79-year-old woman. It revealed quite a lot about John and how he thought. I don't know if he felt more disappointed or flattered when I expressed how much I loved it. It remains a favorite of mine to this day.

Afterward, I revealed my own cinematic wonder— *The Lion King*. He fussed and fumed and protested that he wasn't watching any baby movie (I later learned that he had *never* seen a Disney movie). But I had already watched his choice. And a deal was a deal. So we watched. He slumped back with a disdainful look as the castle appeared and Tinkerbell swirled around it to "When You Wish Upon a Star" during the opening credits.

The next time I glanced over at him, he was wide eyed, his face responding unwittingly to every turn in the plot. When Mufasa died in the canyon, he actually blurted out an imploring "No!" despite himself. He stealthily dried his eyes on his sleeve. I did the same, but for different reasons.

I began to help John with school work and he passed tenth grade somehow. With the onset of summer, I took John to the beach—another first for him at sixteen. The issue of wearing shorts was no mean hurdle, but I finally managed to cajole him into cutting a pair of his older black jeans into something at least in the ballpark. He wore them to the beach with a leather belt.

Reaching the shore involved passing through several more towns John had never been in, and we named them off as we passed the borders of each, causing him to feel like quite the seasoned traveler. As we neared the beach, he noticed the difference in the tree line and smelled the salt in the air, commenting with no little wonder at these things.

Finally, we arrived. His eyes were large, darting around to take it all in. The parking lot, that is, as the ocean itself was still obscured from view by the dunes. I felt like a father watching his young son learn to walk as John's feet hit the sand for the first time in his life, struggling to work muscles in ways he'd never had to, navigating his way up the shifting incline uncertainly. Halfway to the top, he heard what lay beyond, roaring and shushing. "Is that… the *ocean?*" I remember him asking incredulously. He really seemed to have no idea that it was only yards away, just out of sight.

And then we crested the dune. The ocean spread out before us. John stood there, unable to keep walking for a moment. He almost seemed confused, overwhelmed, as he took in the foreign scene before him. Then he made a run for it, taking no care for the strips of rocks in his way. He "eeked" and "ouched" his way to the water and splashed right in. "It really *is* salty!" he exclaimed, as if he didn't believe this fact from the books he'd read about it. Suddenly, he pointed as if at a ghost, his mouth agape. Something was moving across the sand. "Is that… a *real crab?*"

John was tasting of innocence and possibility. His world was enlarging. And it was already changing him. He decided that he'd like to try kicking the drugs. He *believed* that he could.

John's mother was anything but happy about the changes in him. She seemed to take his mention of every new adventure as a barb, as though he were gloating instead of merely sharing his new-found happiness. When he told her he was done with drugs, it was the last straw. If he was not going to be her middle man to supporting her own habit more inexpensively, then he was just taking up space and money. She kicked him out.

At first, John hopped from basements to cars to couches, trying to make his way. But he soon realized that he would have no success laying off the drugs when all of his benefactors were users themselves. Still in my twenties, I offered to take John in until he finished high school. He stayed with me for nearly two years, working odd jobs and attending night school.

While with me, he continued to struggle on and off with drinking and drugs. I knew that he really wanted to change; but at every turn, there were people all too willing to share their wares. And it had been his life for a long time. Still, he kept trying.

The first summer John was with me, friends made plans to do a whitewater rafting trip down the Colorado River in the Grand Canyon, and they asked if I'd like to join. I knew I could not really afford the trip, especially now that I had another mouth to feed. And of course, I couldn't leave John by himself for that long. So my first response was that, no, I wouldn't be able to go. But inside, I kept imagining John at the beach that first time. I knew the sight of the Grand Canyon would be stunning for me, even having seen some of the world. But for John? Ten days away, out in nature—and not just *any* nature, but the Grand Canyon. I couldn't get it out of my mind.

Throwing caution to the wind, I held my breath, got out my credit card, and booked us both for the trip.

The plane ride itself was an unimaginable thrill for John. And then, along the road from Albuquerque to Lake Powell, he was further introduced to Native American culture and lizards for the first time. The initial cracks began to appear in the distance—narrow slivers. John was stunned: "Oh, *wow!* It's so *cool!*"

I informed him, with great pleasure and amusement, that we were hours from the actual Canyon yet.

When we did arrive at the first legitimate lookout point, we parked the van and walked to the edge. Here was John, cresting another hill, unaware of what he would see on the other side. And there it was.

Breathtaking.

No postcard or picture can capture the awe of that place. It really can't. Yet, as taken aback as I was, John was suddenly transported to some fantasy land that only existing in movies and dreams. He was transfixed. Transcendent. He swayed a little bit. His eyes glassed over. And then he just wept, falling to his knees, his black jeans kicking up the red dust: "It's… so… *beautiful!*"

The rafting trip and the ten-hour hike out of the Canyon were indescribable, particularly in their effect on John. Here, sleeping out under night skies that held more starlight than blackness between, he was changing yet again.

THE BEST ADVICE SO FAR:
Remind yourself often that
there is *always* more to life.

It was not a straight path from there for John. But it was a *different* one. And I'm happy to say that John made it. Today, he is a hard-working chief mechanic, owner of his own shop. Trusted. Respected. Optimistic. Compassionate. A mentor to many others. And drug free.

I'm a firm believer that there is always something new and wondrous to behold and experience. I don't have the finances to jet set off to African safaris or the Taj Mahal. Dib gave me a book one Christmas a few years back called *1000 Places to See Before You Die* (Schultz, 2003). To date, I have only seen two or three. But it isn't just about the ability to travel to faraway places.

Here are just a handful of things that keep my view of life expanding:

Trying new foods.

Appreciating dance.

Reading and sharing poetry.

Watching Discovery Channel programs.

"Collecting" other languages and using them where I can.

Tucking away new vocabulary words and finding ways to use them.

Listening to music and reading books outside my preferred genres, whether I particularly love them or not.

Learning anything new at all, however minute. An origami fold. The etymology of a word or origin of a phrase. How to tie a particular knot.

Meeting and talking with people who appear at first to be very different from myself. The more diverse, the better.

It's a mindset. It's purposefully keeping a sense of wonder and imagination. And like taking to heart any of the advice presented in this book, it's about getting uncomfortable with the idea of staying in your comfort zone. It's living as if there is more to life than the path I walked yesterday. Because there is.

Much more.

Questions for Reflection and Discussion:

APPENDIX page 407

A Personal Request

Now that you've completed the book, I have a simple request of you: would you leave a review of **_The Best Advice So Far_** on Amazon or GoodReads?

Your review will directly impact the reach that this book is able to have. Reviews are often the number-one reason shoppers will choose a book or pass it by.

And I read each and every review myself; so your review would be a personal encouragement to me as I continue to mentor, write, speak and do all I can to spread positivity, purpose and hope to others.

Thank you!

about the author

ERIK TYLER

Erik is an author, speaker, blogger, mentor, facilitator, people-lover, creative force, conversationalist, problem solver, chance-taker, noticer and lover of life. He lives in the Boston area.

facebook.com/eriktylerauthor

@BestAdviceSoFar

booking@TheBestAdviceSoFar.com

www.TheBestAdviceSoFar.com

APPENDIX

Questions *for* Reflection *and* Discussion

Preface

1. What led to your reading this book? What are your expectations, based on what you know about the book so far?

2. How do you react or respond when someone offers you advice?

3. Do you tend to be someone who seeks advice?

4. What's some of the best advice you've gotten so far? Why do you consider it the best?

5. Are you famous for giving any certain advice often? Do you remember where you first came across this advice?

THE BEST ADVICE SO FAR:
You *always* have a choice.

Chapter 1: Choice

1. You always have a choice. What do you think of this idea? Is this hard for you to accept or believe?

2. In what areas is it most difficult for you to feel that you have a choice?

3. Think about an area where you feel stuck right now. Try to name at least three choices you could make in this situation. What might the results or consequences of each of these choices be? Are those results or consequences certain, likely, possible or imagined?

4. What are some of the benefits of remembering that you always have a choice?

5. Are there any downsides you see to accepting that you always have a choice?

THE BEST ADVICE SO FAR:
Being miserable is a choice.

Chapter 2: Negativity

1. What is your reaction to the idea that "being miserable is a choice"?

2. Do you consider yourself a negative person?

3. Take a risk: ask 3 to 5 people who know you very, "Please be honest with me—do you think of me as a positive or negative person?" Don't debate, argue or cajole. Just listen. Regardless of the answers you receive, ask each person, "What about me makes you say that?" If you are using these questions for group discussion, regardless of whether you know everyone well or not, consider asking the other group members to answer this about you.

4. This chapter suggests that there is always a perceived gain for what we do in life. If you've become negative in a certain area—or in general—what do you think your own perceived gain might be?

5. What do you fear you might lose by committing with others to change patterns of negativity?

6. How might your life change if you were to truly let go of negativity? Imagine a specific area or relationship that would be affected, and then describe the change you imagine might be possible in as much detail as you can within your group, to a friend or in writing.

THE BEST ADVICE SO FAR:
Practice positivity.

Chapter 3: Positivity

1. What do you think of the idea that simply being less negative doesn't necessarily mean that you are a *positive* person?

2. Who is the most genuinely positive person you know? How do you feel when you are around them? Do you find this person inspiring or daunting?

3. Think of one challenging or difficult situation you currently face. Try to name at least one "silver lining" that exists in this situation.

4. How do you feel when challenged to consider the silver lining in difficult situations? Rueful? Sarcastic? Thankful? Cheerful? Neutral? Something else?

5. How drastic a shift would it be for you to *practice* The Silver Lining Game on a regular basis? Does this seem realistic to you?

THE BEST ADVICE SO FAR:
You have to start from where you *are*,
not from where you *wish* you were.

Chapter 4: Starting Again

1. What are some times when you've had to start over in life? How did you handle those times?

2. What are some words or phrases that you associate with starting over?

3. Do you consider yourself a self-motivator when it comes to starting over, or do you fare better with help? If the latter, do you tend to seek out that help when you need it, or to avoid starting over instead?

4. Is there any area where you'd presently like to start over? What holds you back?

THE BEST ADVICE SO FAR:
The sooner you realize
that life is not fair,
the happier you will be.

Chapter 5: Unfairness

1. Can you think of a person in your own life who tends to see life as categorically unfair to them? How do you feel when you spend time in the company of this person?

2. Are there circumstances you feel or have felt to be unfair about your life?

3. When things seem unfair in your own life, how do you tend to respond?

4. When you advise a friend or family member who is feeling that life is unfair, what might you be likely to say? How closely does your advice to others match your personal reactions when your own life seems unfair?

5. Can you think of a specific time when you reacted well to unfair circumstances? How do you think your choices affected the events that followed?

THE BEST ADVICE SO FAR:
If you're expecting someone else
to make you happy,
you never will be.

Chapter 6: Happiness

1. What do you think are some tell-tale signs that we might be relying on others for our own happiness?

2. Be honest: Are you currently letting your happiness hinge on someone else's actions or responses to you? If not, have you ever?

3. What are the perceived benefits of letting others make you happy? What are the drawbacks?

4. Consider the central piece of advice in this chapter: **"If you're expecting someone else to make you happy, you never will be."** Is this concept a new one for you to consider? Do you think it is sound advice? If not, what problems do you see with it?

5. What is your personal response to the related claim that "...no one can *make* you mad. Or jealous "? Do you agree or disagree? Why?

6. How difficult a change would it be for you at this point in your life to apply the advice from this chapter? What realistic first step would you need to take in order to put it into practice?

THE BEST ADVICE SO FAR:
It's not all that important for people
to know that you know.

Chapter 7: The Limelight/Stealing

1. Think of a specific person you know whom you would consider a "limelight stealer." What is your attitude toward this person? How do you respond when this person is around you and begins to steal the limelight?

2. Are there times when you yourself tend to steal the limelight, or are tempted to, by one-upping others or being sure they "know that you know"? Can you recall the specifics of a time when you stole the limelight?

3. Has anyone ever actually *told* you that you stole the limelight after the fact? How did they express this to you?

4. Can you identify at all with being a "silent" limelight stealer, through smug or condescending looks or attitudes?

5. What do you think about the advice to consider whether what you feel compelled to share will have any negative effects if you don't say it, or any positive effects if you do? Does this seem practical or unrealistic to you?

THE BEST ADVICE SO FAR:
Make it your goal to foster
others-centered moments as opposed to
me-centered moments.

Chapter 8: The Limelight/Sharing

1. Think of a specific person you know whom you would consider an active "limelight sharer." What is your attitude toward this person? How do you respond when this person is around you?

2. Would you consider yourself an active "limelight sharer"? On what do you base your answer?

3. What is your honest reaction to the use of the terms "others-centered moments" and "me-centered moments"?

4. What is the last specific and sincere compliment you received? Who gave it? How did you know it was sincere? How did you feel?

5. What is the last specific and sincere compliment you gave? To whom did you give it? What was their reaction?

6. Are you someone who thanks people specifically and often? If not, why do you think this is the case?

7. As you consider the conversation tools of asking, reflecting and inviting, where would you place yourself on a scale of 1 (terrible) to 10 (terrific)? Do you feel some people just naturally have these skills? Or do you believe they can be developed by anyone, given practice?

THE BEST ADVICE SO FAR:
Put the power and beauty of a name
to good use.

Chapter 9: Names

1. How many different names (real, variations, nicknames, taunts, titles, etc.) can you recall having been called in your lifetime so far? Which was/is your favorite? Why? Which would you rather not have been called? Why?

2. In your opinion, has the value of speaking others' names been overestimated in this chapter?

3. Do you think, on the whole, the social use of referring to people by name in conversation has changed over time where you live? If so, to what do you attribute this change?

4. What are some generic fill-ins people tend to use socially in place of real names (example: "sir," "guy," "hun," etc.)? Why do you think these fill-ins exist? Are you someone who uses these at all? If so, what are yours?

5. Are you someone who is generally comfortable exchanging names and using names in everyday conversation with strangers? If so, were you always this way; and if you were not naturally this way, what changed? If you are not someone who is comfortable with names, why do you think that is?

6. In the specific example of referring to wait staff at a restaurant by name and giving them your own name in conversation, how comfortable would you be with this right now in your life?

THE BEST ADVICE SO FAR:
Kindness still works.

Chapter 10: Kindness

1. Have you ever been on the receiving end of a Random Act of Kindness from a stranger or someone you did not know well? Relive the details for a moment. How did you react?

2. When was the last time (if ever) that you initiated an intentional act of kindness for a stranger or someone you did not know well? Relive those details for a moment. How did the interaction go, from your perspective and theirs? How did you feel about it afterward?

3. What positive effects do you think it might have on your life if you became intentional and regular about practicing kindness? How would you define "intentional" and "regular" as it pertains to this idea? Can you foresee any negative effects of adopting this mindset and practice?

THE BEST ADVICE SO FAR:
Set clearly-stated, positive expectations
for your relationships.

Chapter 11: Rules Of Engagement

1. What is your initial reaction to the idea of specifically voicing positive expectations in your relationships?

2. Do you think this practice is harder for some subsets of people than others (e.g., men/women, teens/adults, Northerners/Southerners, blue collar/white collar, etc.)? If so, on what do you base that assumption?

3. Think of one person in your life with whom you might particularly like to have positive "ground rules" established? What about your current relationship with this person made you think of them when asked this question?

4. How do you think you would react if someone took you out to dinner and expressed their desire to take their relationship with you to a new place by establishing the kinds of positive expectations described in this chapter? Would this be an awkward conversation for you? Would you feel honored? Relieved? Pressured? Something else?

5. These guidelines are not a magic formula. Are there other positive expectations you think might be a good addition? Would you suggest omitting, rephrasing or otherwise changing any of the three offered in this chapter? If so, which and why?

THE BEST ADVICE SO FAR:
Honesty is not always the best policy.

Chapter 12: Honesty

1. Prior to reading this chapter, would you have said that honesty is always the best policy? Why or why not?

2. Has honesty, however good the intentions, ever gotten you into trouble? If so, recount one specific time this has happened. Looking back, would you have done anything differently?

3. What are some self-serving reasons you or others might employ direct honesty? What are some noble or altruistic reasons you or others might employ direct honesty?

4. How easy or difficult is it for you at this point to look beyond what someone is asking to why they might be asking it? Do you think this skill is innate, learned through practice, or a combination of the two?

5. A short, three-point checklist was offered on the last page of this chapter, as a means of deciding if what you are about to say really needs to be said. It was followed by this question: "Think of your interactions in the last day or so. Using this screening process, what *wouldn't* you have said?" How would you answer this question?

THE BEST ADVICE SO FAR:
Learn to listen as well as you speak.

Chapter 13: Conversation

1. When it comes to conversation, are you someone who tends to draw others out, someone who needs to be drawn out, or neither?

2. When there is silence in a conversation, what do you typically do?

3. Who is one person with whom you'd really like to have more comfortable and fulfilling conversations?

4. Of the five suggested approaches to conversation mentioned in this chapter, which do you feel you are best at right now? Which seems the most challenging for you?

5. This chapter offers a lot of information, but that can sometimes feel overwhelming. What is one small first step that you could take toward improving your active listening and communication skills?

THE BEST ADVICE SO FAR:
Tenacious love expressed with creativity
can work wonders.

Chapter 14: Creative Love

1. What is your initial reaction to the story of Ricky?

2. This chapter is entitled "CREATIVE LOVE." Do you feel love *must* be creative in order to be effective? Is it possible to have real love that is uncreative?

3. Do you feel that only "creative people" can be creative in loving others? Or do you feel that being intentional about loving someone naturally results in greater creativity? (Neither? Both?)

4. Reflect on a specific time when someone showed you what you would consider "creative love." Who was the person? What were the circumstances? What makes you qualify this act as "creative"? Would you consider this person creative in general?

5. Who is someone in your own life who you feel could use some creative love lately?

THE BEST ADVICE SO FAR:
Patience is still a virtue.

Chapter 15: Patience

1. Who is the most patient person you know? Have they always been this patient, or was patience something they developed over time?

2. If ten people who know you well were anonymously asked to describe you as either "patient" or "impatient" by clicking one or the other in a simple online survey, what do you think your score would come back as (considering that you get 10% for each person who clicks "patient")?

3. In what areas of life do you find yourself becoming impatient most often? What do you think it is about this particular type of situation that triggers your impatience?

4. Can you think of one practical way to build patience into this area of your life?

THE BEST ADVICE SO FAR:
Don't just *not plan* to get into trouble;
plan *not to* get into trouble.

Chapter 16: Avoiding Trouble

1. If we're honest, we all get ourselves into trouble sometimes. Do you tend to get into trouble more through things you do, things you say or things you think?

2. From your perspective, is it easier to change behaviors, words or thoughts?

3. When was the last time you found yourself in trouble of your own doing? How far ahead did you see it coming, if at all?

4. In this area, what is something you could have done to "plan not to get into trouble" rather than just "not plan to get into trouble"? If you are discussing with a group, try brainstorming ways to avoid specific kinds of trouble.

THE BEST ADVICE SO FAR:
A fire with no fuel quickly goes out.

Chapter 17: Drama

1. Try completing this short definition in your own words: "Drama is _____."

2. Complete this sentence with an action or attitude: "People who love drama tend to _____."

3. Are you someone who secretly (or perhaps not so secretly) enjoys or perpetuates drama?

4. Can you think of a personal situation where the central advice from this chapter did not (or would not) work? What about this situation do you think negates this advice?

5. What difference is there, if any, between "not throwing fuel on a fire" and ignoring a real problem? Should both situations be treated essentially the same way? Explain your answer.

THE BEST ADVICE SO FAR:
Motive is more important
than behavior or outcome.

Chapter 18: Motives

1. Do you agree or disagree with the central advice from this chapter, that motive is more important than behavior or outcome? On what do you base your answer?

2. Most of us can quickly think of legal situations in which behavior is more important than motive, in the sense that the punishment is based on the behavior rather than the motive. Technicalities of the legal system aside, can you think of a specific interpersonal situation in which behavior is, in fact, more important than motive?

3. Think of a current or recent situation where someone's behavior really upset you. Now imagine that your job is to be this person's defense lawyer. Brainstorm any possible motives which may have been less than diabolical (i.e., positive, neutral, ignorant, etc.), yet which could account for this person's behavior. If you are discussing these questions with a group, have one member share a situation where someone's behavior really upset them, and have the rest of the group offer possible "defenses" of this person's motives.

THE BEST ADVICE SO FAR:
When conversations become difficult,
being aware of physical changes and
reporting them openly can
help calm things down.

Chapter 19: Vital Signs

1. Are you someone who tends to be aware of your own physical reactions during times of conflict or stress?

2. Doctors and medical staff are trained to ask us simple questions in order to find out what our symptoms are during times of illness. How difficult do you think it would be for you to learn to ask *yourself* simple diagnostic questions during times of conflict or stress, and to answer those questions clearly aloud.

THE BEST ADVICE SO FAR:
When you have a potentially
controversial topic at hand,
throw a bone first.

Chapter 20: Softening Blows

1. How does the idea of "throwing a bone" before delivering a potentially controversial message strike you?

2. How difficult is it for you to think of and offer a positive, related and sincere compliment when you feel angry, threatened or disappointed?

3. What might we lose by "throwing a bone" before delivering a tough message to someone? What stands to be gained by doing so?

4. "Throwing a bone" is an others-centered practice when done with right motive. But in what ways could learning to soften blows benefit you yourself, as well?

THE BEST ADVICE SO FAR:
Asking the right kind of questions works better than making statements.

Chapter 21: Asking Questions

1. Do you tend to ask good questions or make strong statements most often?

2. By way of review, can you recall from the chapter some of the types of less-than-useful questions?

3. Do you know anyone personally who you would consider to be an especially good question asker?

4. Several benefits of using thoughtful questions instead of statements were discussed in this chapter. Can you think of any additional benefits that were not mentioned?

THE BEST ADVICE SO FAR:
You can't demand respect.
You have to earn it.

Chapter 22: Respect

1. Were any of your existing ideas challenged while reading this chapter?

2. Have you ever had someone demand that you respect them? What was/is your reaction to this person? In short, did their demands for respect work?

3. Have you ever demanded respect from someone? What was this person's reaction to you? Again, in short, did it work?

4. Who is someone in your life whom it is hard for you to respect? Why? What would it take for them to earn your respect?

5. Who is someone in your life whose respect you wish you could earn? What do you think it will take to earn this person's respect?

THE BEST ADVICE SO FAR:
Clipped weeds soon return.

Chapter 23: Compliance

1. Let's start with a broad question: what is your reaction to the ideas presented in this chapter? Did you have any particularly strong positive or negative reactions?

2. Can you think of any relationships where forced compliance is necessary, regardless of consideration for underlying issues that may exist? Is there a common element that characterizes such relationships?

3. Can you recall any personal circumstances where compliance was gained but the "weeds" were still clearly evidenced later?

4. Can you identify any relationships in your life right now where you are attempting to enforce compliance without having adequately considered the underlying causes or future effects?

THE BEST ADVICE SO FAR:
Focus on the person not the problem.

Chapter 24: People vs. Problems

1. How would you have reacted if Jerry had "done his deed" in *your* classroom (assuming you were the teacher)?

2. How does the central piece of advice from this chapter parallel the advice from CHAPTER 18: MOTIVES (**"The Best Advice So Far: Motive is more important than behavior or outcome"**)? How do the two pieces of advice differ?

3. Is there anyone in your life right now whom you've been treating as a problem rather than as a person? What are some positive characteristics about this person, or hopes you have for them outside of "the problem" as it relates to you?

4. What is one way you can be intentional in your interactions with the person you chose above, so that they will feel like you see them as a person and not as a problem?

THE BEST ADVICE SO FAR:
Whatever you choose to do,
do it without expectations,
simply because you believe in doing it.

Chapter 25: Expectations

1. Bring to mind a time when you invested considerable time and energy into a project or endeavor (not an individual person just yet), and things did not turn out as you had planned. Was the outcome better or worse than you expected?

2. What sort of conversations did you have with others (or what sort of self-dialog) when things did not turn out as you had planned in the situation above? In other words, how did you verbalize your feelings about it to others or to yourself? What kinds of words did you use?

3. Did the outcome of the events above deter you from getting involved in similar endeavors afterward? For how long? Still?

4. In this book, the idea of "perceived gain" is discussed. What was your perceived gain in investing time and energy into the endeavor above? In other words, what was your motivation for doing it?

5. Now think of a person into whom you've invested a considerable amount of time and energy, yet with whom things did not turn out as you had hoped. Go back and respond to Questions 2, 3 and 4 above, with this person in mind.

6. What kind of mindset change(s) would be necessary in order for you to invest fully again in people or situations similar to the ones above?

THE BEST ADVICE SO FAR:
Humility is a strength, not a weakness.

Chapter 26: Humility

1. Prior to reading this chapter, was your perception of the concept of humility a largely positive or negative one? For what reason(s)? Has your perception changed or been challenged at all after having read this chapter?

2. According to the viewpoint offered in this chapter, can a person be extremely talented or good looking, confident, extroverted or hold a position of leadership and still be humble? What might cause you to think of such a person as truly humble?

3. According to this chapter, humility does not mean always deferring to what others want, being afraid to speak up, or allowing yourself to be mistreated. Have you ever confused humility with this type of behavior, in yourself or in others?

4. Who is someone you've always considered to be humble? When viewed in light of the definition of humility offered in this chapter, would you still say this person is humble?

5. As viewed in light of this chapter, do you consider yourself a humble person in general? Are there people you are more humble with than others? If so, why do you think that is the case?

THE BEST ADVICE SO FAR:
Putting awkwardness out there
on the table by calling it what it is
immediately takes most of the
awkwardness out of it.

Chapter 27: Awkwardness

1. What are some of the most awkward moments you can remember from your life thus far ("thus far" because you can be assured of having more)?

2. As you remember or recount these awkward moments now, what is your *current* reaction to them? Do they seem every bit as bad as they seemed at the time? Worse? Funnier? Other?

3. What has been your typical reaction when something awkward happens? Why do you think you have this reaction?

4. On a scale of 1 to 10, where 1 = Excited and 10 = Utterly Horrified, how does the thought of **"putting awkwardness out there on the table by calling it what it is"** strike you?

5. Go back to a situation you mentioned in Question 1 above. What do you *imagine* would have happened if you'd put the awkward thing out there by voicing it openly? Now pretend you get a cash prize if you are able to come up with at least one realistic positive outcome that may have happened if you'd voiced the awkwardness; what might such a realistic positive outcome have been?

THE BEST ADVICE SO FAR:
Apologize less and mean it more.

Chapter 28: Apologies

1. If you had to choose one or the other, would you say you are someone who tends to apologize too much, or too little?

2. Did/do you have good role models where apologies are concerned?

3. Why do you think it is so difficult for people to apologize when they know they are in the wrong? Why do you think it is so tempting for people to apologize when they don't mean it?

4. This book makes no claim to have figured everything out, or to be the end-all-be-all of truth and wisdom. Are there any parts of this chapter with which you disagree? Why?

5. Are there any specific thoughts from this chapter that you found to ring true and be a personal challenge where apologies are concerned?

.

THE BEST ADVICE SO FAR:
"No" is a complete answer.

Chapter 29: Saying No

1. Do you have a hard time saying no? If so, why do you think it's so hard for you?

2. Do you have a particularly *easy* time saying no? If so, do you think people ask you to do less because of it? Do you feel people take your "no" as rude or just matter-of-fact?

3. In saying no, do you ever struggle with the impulse to over-explain why you are saying no?

4. Think of a recent time when you said yes, but should have said no. What were the particular reasons you said yes to this person? What do you think would have happened had you said no, both personally and in terms of the task or event you would have declined?

5. How do you feel after reading this chapter about the idea of simply but kindly saying no and leaving it at that?

THE BEST ADVICE SO FAR:
Decide never to duck around
corners in life.

Chapter 30: Avoidance

1. Be brutally honest: regardless of when you last actually saw them, is there someone you'd rather avoid? What are some words that describe how you feel about running into this person?

2. Three possible reasons for avoiding someone were suggested in this chapter. Can you think of any others that these three don't cover?

3. Think of the person you brought to mind above. Which of the three reasons, if any, best describes the reason you'd rather avoid the person?

4. What is your reaction as you envision taking the specific approach offered in this chapter toward deciding not to duck from this person moving forward? Fill in this blank: "Taking that advice will be _____ for me."

THE BEST ADVICE SO FAR:
Sometimes, it's better to run
from a beast than to try to tame it.

Chapter 31: Bowing Out

1. The "beasts" referred to in this chapter are voluntary "extras" we take on in life, which gradually take over, using up our energy and joy. Are there any beasts roaming around in your life right now?

2. How did this activity or undertaking seem to you at first? Why did you originally get involved? What changed?

3. How do you distinguish between an activity or undertaking that you should stick with a while longer even though it's hard, and a beast?

4. What do you *imagine* will happen if you kick your particular beast out? How does that compare with what reason tells you will *likely* happen?

5. Envision yourself two weeks after putting your beast out for good. How does your life look from there?

THE BEST ADVICE SO FAR:
When it comes to loss,
keep it sincere and simple.

Chapter 32: Condolences

1. Do you find it hard to know what to say to people during times of loss, or do you generally feel comfortable with what to say during such times?

2. Do you see yourself in any of the cautionary examples from this chapter?

3. During times of loss in your own life, what kinds of responses have you found personally most helpful? How did your relationship with the other person change your perception of what they offered by way of condolences?

4. Do you agree or disagree with the particular advice centering on the example of sitting next to a severely burned person on a bus? Why?

5. Did any of the suggestions as to "what not to do" from this chapter strike a particular chord with you?

THE BEST ADVICE SO FAR:
Worry serves no purpose but to ruin the present.

Chapter 33: Worry

1. Do you consider yourself a worrier?

2. Do you think worrying is something we learn and, therefore, can change? Or do you think that worrying is just a part of some people's personality which is beyond their control?

3. A challenge was issued early on in this chapter: "Try to come up with one positive thing that worry accomplishes." Can you?

4. Do you have any effective strategies already in place for dealing with worry? How consistent are you in using them, if so? What are your thoughts on the "screening questions" presented in this chapter as a means of banishing worry?

THE BEST ADVICE SO FAR:
When negative emotions are strong,
discipline yourself to think in specifics
rather than extremes.

Chapter 34: Extremes

1. Can you think of a recent time you spoke in extremes: never, always, no one, everyone, nothing, everything, etc.? If you were to be specific and remove the extreme words, what was it that was actually bothering you?

2. If you are in a discussion group as you consider these questions right now, try some role playing. Take turns having one person throw out an extreme statement while others ask focused questions that help this person remove the extremes and get to the specific issue underneath.

THE BEST ADVICE SO FAR:
You can always do more—
and *less*—than you thought
you could do.

Chapter 35: Limitations

1. Would you say that you more tend to do *less* than you are capable of doing, or that you struggle with constantly trying to do *more* than you should?

2. What are some possible underlying causes of chronic underachievement? Are any of these true of you? How might you best address the things that hold you back from your potential?

3. Many people don't seem to understand fully that being an overachiever can have significantly negative effects on a person, even though outwardly that person is often perceived in a positive light. If you are an overachiever, try to describe (to the group or on paper to yourself) any negative effects that constantly trying to do more has had on you.

4. How do you react to the idea that, without you and what you do in the world, the world will go on? Is this discouraging? Why do *anything*, if the world will go on without your doing it?

THE BEST ADVICE SO FAR:
Don't color the present with the past.

Chapter 36: Past vs. Present

1. Think of one specific area where you have allowed (or are currently allowing) the past to color the present. If you've told yourself that these two things are "just like" one another, can you name a few differences between them?

2. This chapter is not suggesting that you just give yourself a pep talk before facing a situation that seems similar to a past one, or that you grit your teeth and just plow through it. How is doing either of those things different from what is presented in this chapter?

3. What is your biggest personal obstacle to separating the past from the present? What positive step could you take toward overcoming that obstacle?

THE BEST ADVICE SO FAR:
Cultivate silence in your life.

Chapter 37: Silence

1. Are you comfortable with silence? Are you intentional about cultivating silence in your life?

2. Who is someone you know who *does* cultivate silence in their life? How would you describe this person?

3. In an average week, not counting time you are asleep, how long would you estimate that you currently experience intentional silence?

4. If you can remember, what sorts of thoughts tend to emerge during times when you are silent (e.g., while you are in bed, before you have fallen asleep)?

5. What scares you about leaving room for silence and reflection in your life? What benefits do you think could come of it in your own life?

6. Is there one time slot in your current schedule that you could turn into a time for cultivating silence if you were intentional?

THE BEST ADVICE SO FAR:
Do something new every day.

Chapter 38: Boredom

1. How often do you find yourself feeling bored?

2. What do you think about the suggestion that "most boredom is just laziness in disguise"?

3. What factors do you think turn the creativity of childhood into boredom as we get older?

4. Pretend you get a $100,000 prize if you can name five new things you could have done or tried today. Would you win the prize? (Prove it.)

5. What is one new thing you will commit to try by tomorrow?

THE BEST ADVICE SO FAR:
Never pass a lemonade stand
without stopping.

Chapter 39: Lemonade

1. What adjectives come to mind when you consider the thought of (or actually see) kids running a lemonade stand?

2. Simple question: do you stop? If you do not tend to stop, what sort of mental dialog goes on as you pass by, if any?

3. This chapter is about more than deciding to stop at lemonade stands. What do you think the bigger ideas of this chapter are meant to be?

THE BEST ADVICE SO FAR:
Laugh.

Chapter 40: Laughter

1. So... when *was* the last time you laughed so hard that you cried, your stomach hurt, or you couldn't catch your breath?

2. Have you ever had a sustained and utterly ridiculous episode of laughter that compared with "Kermit's Closet"?

3. If it's been a while since you really belly laughed, why do you think that is? Did you used to laugh more at some time in the past? If so, what was it about that time that differs from now?

4. Why do you think laughter has been compared to medicine?

5. In general, why do you think adults laugh less often than children do? Is this par for the course—something we just need to accept? Or is it something we can change? Should we?

THE BEST ADVICE SO FAR:
Stay childlike.

Chapter 41: Being an Adult

1. Reminisce a bit. What are a few things you loved to do when you were a kid?

2. What was it that kept you from doing these things after a certain point in your life? Were they good reasons to stop?

3. What do you think about the suggestion that time seems to go faster as we get older because we stop living in the present and start marking our lives in future deadlines?

4. Do you think you would enjoy some of your favorite childhood activities if you tried them again *now*? What if a few of your closest friends were in on it? Would that change your perspective?

5. What do you think the difference is, if any, between being childish and being childlike?

THE BEST ADVICE SO FAR:
Never lose your sense of wonder.

Chapter 42: Wonder

1. We use the verb form of "wonder " somewhat regularly (e.g., "I wonder what's keeping Joe."); but we don't often use the noun form. What are some synonyms for the noun form of "wonder"? (For those who are a little rusty with grammar, synonyms are other words that mean the same thing.)

2. Are you able to recall the sense of wonder at things when you were younger? What do you think causes the shift to losing that sense of wonder as we get older?

3. When is the last time you explored (an area, the woods, your attic, the Internet): *truly* explored, for the express purpose of finding out something you don't already know or have not seen?

4. What do you think about the idea that taking ourselves too seriously is one of the thieves of wonder?

5. What practical steps could you take that might begin to restore your sense of wonder?

THE BEST ADVICE SO FAR:
Remind yourself often that
there is *always* more to life.

Chapter 43: Going Beyond

1. When was the last time you would say you were truly awe-struck by something (in a positive way)?

2. Sometimes, we can get into ruts where even our leisure activities are chosen from a small set of predictable options. How often do you break your routine?

3. Do you have a "bucket list"? If so, what are some of the things on it? How many have you achieved so far? Are you intentional about doing them, or are they more like pipedreams?

4. If you do not have a "bucket list," why not? In this moment, can you think of at least one thing that you've always wanted to do or try, a place you've wanted to visit? What would it take to make that a reality?

5. You've made it to the end of this book. What will you choose to do differently from here?

You always have a choice — at the very least a choice of response

Made in the USA
Monee, IL
30 April 2023

32745553R10236